BUCKET

~ TO ~

GREECE

Volume 4

V.D. BUCKET

Editor: James Scraper
Cover: German Creative
Interior Format: The Book Khaleesi

Other Books in the
Bucket to Greece Series

Chapter 1

An Overstayed Welcome

"Ouzo, Raki, Mythos," I counted aloud, attempting to identify the tail end of a scruffy orange specimen grubbing around in the dirt, straining to peck at some green beans growing too close to the netting.

"I don't mind if I do, make mine a Mythos," Barry said cheerily, joining me at the bottom of the garden and swatting away a pesky mosquito. Closing his eyes Barry inhaled the fragrant air, redolent with the heady scent of rosemary and thyme. "That's better than filling my lungs with sawdust; it's dusty work over in Nektar."

"I'm trying to do a chicken count. Marigold's only gone and named our feathered friends after popular drinks, but it's just confusing things. Ouzo is the spitting image of Mavrodaphni so I may have counted her twice," I clarified. "I'm sure we're missing another one."

"You think a fox has got in?" Barry asked, scanning the netting for signs of forced entry.

"There's no feathery evidence." I recalled the splattered mess I'd confronted the last time a fox created havoc in the chicken run. "The missing one may simply have taken refuge inside the hen house if Cynthia's mutant cat has been on the prowl again. I swear the foul creature takes an unnatural feline delight in tormenting the live-stock."

Biting his bottom lip and rolling his eyes, Barry offered an apology. "I'm sorry about the cat, but I couldn't expect Cynthia to abandon the thing, she's very fond of it for some inexplicable reason."

"Tell that to Marigold, she's not happy that she's had to lock Clawsome and Catastrophe away in my study to spare them from the ardent advances of Cynthia's deviant tom," I groaned, thinking how absurd it was that we were actually giving houseroom to the loathed feline.

"But you've had them seen to, it's not as though Kouneli's attentions are going to result in another litter of kittens," Barry argued.

"That's hardly the point Barry, his attentions are obviously unwanted. The persistent purrvert has an uncouth approach to courting that leaves Marigold's imports cowering, they are delicate creatures after all," I protested.

"I know," Barry conceded. "I'm sorry to put you in this position Victor, I really must find somewhere else for us to live pretty sharpish. You can cut the tension between Cynthia and Marigold with a knife up in the kitchen, though they make the pretence that everything is hunky-dory. If things go on like this we may not even make it to the wedding."

I nodded in agreement, ruminating over our current dilemma. After just two weeks of living under the same roof, Marigold and Cynthia were so icily polite to each other that the temperate in their presence plummeted to freezing despite the July heat. Barry had finally 'up-sticked' to Meli the previous month, moving in with his fiancée Cynthia and enthusiastically throwing himself into building work with his new business partner Vangelis, the local builder.

Barry and Cynthia had only been ensconced in her cosy love nest for a week when the landlady gave notice they must quit the rented house by the end of the month. By the time Stan rolled up in the removal van crammed with all Barry's worldly belongings there was no point in unpacking; instead his stuff was now gathering dust, stashed away in our downstairs storage space. Naturally Marigold insisted Barry and Cynthia must move in with us if they hadn't found another place by eviction day, not an easy task since the long hours they were both putting in prior to the wedding left little free time for house hunting, hence their current presence in our spare bedroom.

"I don't really get it," Barry said. "We all get along fine, but there's a definite atmosphere."

"Women can get very territorial in the kitchen," I reasoned.

"Aye, that'll be it," Barry agreed.

"Have you given any more thought to buying Harold's place?" I asked.

"I had a tentative word yesterday, but the obnoxious oik isn't prepared to budge on the price, and I'm not willing to pay the full whack when it will cost a small fortune to rip out all his hideous modern improvements and replace them with traditional features," Barry said.

"There must be a way to handle Harold, after all we both know he's desperate to sell up and move back to old Blighty," I replied, pondering a way to get one over on the vile ex-pat during negotiations. In the circumstances I was beginning to regret being so vocally condescending about the ghastly purple shag-pile, at least to Harold's face.

To Barry's dismay his intended had been adamant there was no way she was prepared to make her home in our downstairs storage. She gave short shrift to his sketches showing how the space could be converted into a delightful abode; putting her foot down she'd told him the wedding was off if he seriously expected her to live underneath his sister and share a garden with her prospective in-laws. Now, after two weeks of suffering Cynthia under our roof, I had to concede she had a valid point about the perils of in-laws living in such close proximity.

Surprisingly it was Cynthia who first mooted the suggestion of buying Harold's house, with the proviso the swimming pool she disapproved of was turned into some kind of weed infested ecological pond with floating lily pads. Her idea had legs; with a bit of imagination Harold's house represented a prize piece of village square real-estate and was certainly habitable enough to live in whilst Barry ripped out the modern touches and restored it to its traditional glory. The newly engaged couple duly viewed the property; Cynthia, like Marigold, certainly had the imagination to see past all Harold and Joan's clutter, though she was amazed how much junk they'd managed to amass in their almost four years in Greece. Only Harold's stubborn reluctance to deal with Barry put a spanner in the works, a reluctance no doubt driven by Barry's hitherto undisguised contempt for the loathed British neighbour.

"Victor, I've brought you some repellent to rub on your exposed bits, you know how the mossies like to feast on you at this time of day," Marigold called out, crinkling her nose in obvious disgust as she got a whiff of the smell emanating from the chicken coop. Guzim had been a tad remiss lately in collecting the droppings to flog as compost; I would need to have words with the Albanian shed dweller.

"I've told Victor he should try vinegar, all the old dears in the village recommend it and I find it works a treat," Barry suggested.

"I had quite enough of going around smelling like a chip shop when I cheffed in the taverna." I retorted.

"Well I brought you a cold beer Barry, not vinegar, though I have to say a sprinkling of vinegar may improve the smell of the chickens," Marigold chuckled, passing her brother a bottle of cold Mythos and thrusting an unwelcome jar of Marmite into my hand. "I have some juicy gossip."

"Juicy gossip, do spill the beans," I encouraged.

"Well apparently Harold was done again last night for drunk driving, word is he's lost his licence for six months this time on top of the hefty fine," Marigold revealed.

"About time, he's a liability on the road," I said with untrammelled delight. "How did you hear about it?"

"I was out on the balcony and heard Harold and Joan tearing two bells out of one another on the street below, so vulgar. I think they must have walked back to the village, Joan was carrying her heels and Harold looked so disreputable I'm sure he must have spent another night in the cells," Marigold said gleefully. Before heading back to the kitchen she cast a contemplative eye over Raki as though sizing the chicken up for the cooking pot.

"We should strike while the iron's hot," Barry suggested.

"Well I'm not wringing its neck," I said adamantly.

"I thought we could start off with a bit of negotiation, rather than violence," Barry said.

"Oh, you mean Harold," I said, realising we had been speaking at cross purposes. "I'm definitely up for a bit of negotiating this evening. If we can handle him right the house could be yours for a handsome discount, there's no way Harold will be able to tolerate living in Meli another minute with no way of getting to the bars on the coast."

"And a cash back-hander may come in handy for the fine he's just been landed with. Perhaps we should arm ourselves with some Mythos and get him plastered," Barry suggested.

"First lubricate our prey, butter him up by sympathising with his predicament, and then move in for the kill by taking advantage of the drunken sap, I like it," I said.

"Let's pop over right now, before dinner. If it goes our way we can hopefully present the ladies with a fait accompli before they kill one another," Barry said.

"Sounds like a plan Barry. By the way it's

good to see how committed you are to improving your Greek language skills."

Furrowing his brow Barry asked, "*Ti?*" What?

"*Fait accompli*. It's the same in Greek," I assured Barry.

"I suppose you've added it to your list of memorised Greek words," my brother-in-law laughed, aware of my proclivity for expanding my Greek vocabulary base with words that were conveniently the same in translation.

"Come on, let's head off to Harold's place, we can stop on the way and stock up on beer at the shop," I urged.

"We may achieve the desired result a bit quicker if we oil the wheels, so to speak, with that bottle of excellent Grouse in your kitchen," Barry proposed.

Turning towards the house we were distracted by the sight of Guzim's pet rabbit and floppy-eared bed fellow bolting across the garden at a reckless speed. Cynthia's mutant cat chased after in hot pursuit, with Guzim hot on the heels of the predatory feline. The Albanian hurled himself on the ground, seizing hold of Kouneli's tail triumphantly. Spitting on the cat he unleashed a torrent of gutturally accented expletives. Clawing its captor, the cat broke free from Guzim's grasp; having lost sight of the rabbit it turned its malicious attentions on my chicken coop.

"*Diavolos gata,*" Guzim shouted. He'd get no argument from me since I was in total agreement that Cynthia's cherished pet was indeed the devil cat. Guzim launched into a long and passionate tirade, speaking so quickly I only managed to recognise every third word. At Guzim's sudden reference to Fatos Nano I made an educated guess that he was claiming it was as unnatural for the cat to want to mate with the rabbit as it was for me to be so infatuated with the handsomeness of the Albanian prime minister; Guzim never seemed to tire of bringing the subject up. If pressed to translate the rest of his outburst I'd hazard a guess that Guzim was venting the opinion that Cynthia's cat had outstayed its welcome. I empathised; all too aware that Marigold considered Cynthia too had outstayed her welcome, though my wife would never resort to such colourful language and would simply soldier on through the icy atmosphere with a stiff upper lip, rather than risk offending Barry.

With Barry's nuptials hanging in the balance the urgency of the situation was apparent. The sooner Barry and I could get Harold inebriated

enough to sign away his house for a much reduced price, the sooner normality would be restored to the Bucket household.

Chapter 2

Under the Influence

Barry and I strolled across the village square, the leafy plane trees offering welcome shade from the still hot sun. Marigold and Cynthia had declined to join us, saying it was too much to expect them to stomach Harold just before dinner, Cynthia trusting us to barter a deal. "Remember he's had no luck schmoozing potential house buyers so don't be stingy pouring the scotch," Marigold had reminded us as she waved us off.

"It's a crying shame to waste such expensive

scotch on Harold," I lamented to Barry, convinced the bottle of methylated spirits I kept under the kitchen sink would serve the same purpose as whisky, Harold being such a boorish ignoramus. "I just hope we can pull this off. The wedding is in less than two weeks and we've already got a houseful of guests flying over."

"I don't suppose you could persuade Violet Burke to bed down in the stone shed with Guzim," Barry joked.

"As irritating as Guzim can be, I still wouldn't inflict my mother on him," I replied. A sudden thought occurred to me; if Barry and Cynthia were still in residence when our overseas guests arrived perhaps I could persuade Guzim to give up his hovel as the honeymoon suite since we didn't have enough bedrooms to accommodate Benjamin and Adam, and Violet Burke, on top of Barry and Cynthia. Unfortunately I realised there was no way Cynthia would go for it even if Guzim was bribable, she didn't strike me as the type to tolerate showering under an outdoor hosepipe.

"Well here we are, I'll jiggle the bottle around as an incentive for him to let us in," Barry said, raising the Union Jack embellished knocker on Harold's front door. "I'll definitely be binning this knocker if he accepts my offer, talk about crass."

Following a lengthy wait Harold thrust the door open, clearly annoyed by the disturbance. Averting my eyes from the grotesque sight of the diminutive and rotund Brit squashed into too tight budgie smugglers, I stared in fascination at the droplets of water dripping over his beer belly; it appeared we had disturbed Harold's pool time.

"This isn't a very convenient time to just turn up, Joan's in the middle of cooking our dinner," Harold said, folding his arms in an unwelcoming pose as we recoiled from the stench of his beery breath.

"We won't take up too much of your time, but we'd like to seriously discuss the sale of the house – perhaps over a glass of this excellent Grouse," I replied, Barry waving the bottle and nodding enthusiastically by my side.

"Grouse you say, you'd best come through. Wipe your feet, I don't want any village muck getting on the shag-pile," Harold invited. Our reluctant host led us through to the pool area, pausing in the kitchen to retrieve some glasses for the Grouse, cheering up considerably when we protested we'd be content with beer. "Put the dinner on hold for now, these two gents are here to discuss business," Harold instructed his wife, sliding his arms into a gaudy Hawaiian shirt that strained to cover most of his gut.

Joan's bat wings visibly wobbled as she hovered over the stove stirring the contents of a pan. A dribble of tomato sauce oozing from one of two open tins of Heinz baked beans complemented Joan's peeling red skin, of which there was far too much on display, bulging from the sheer wrap she'd thrown over her age inappropriate bathing suit. The discarded tins indicated dinner wouldn't spoil by the wait.

"Are you here about the house?" Joan asked.

Replying in the affirmative we intercepted Harold mouthing to his wife to "tidy upstairs" whilst she clearly mouthed back "make sure you sell it."

Out on the patio Barry poured Harold a very generous measure of my Famous Grouse. Not wishing to overplay our hand we perched on a couple of damp sun loungers in contemplative silence, waiting for the whisky to mellow Harold's mood before getting down to business. The sound of Joan pushing a vacuum cleaner around upstairs soon drowned out the trilling song of the cicadas in the nearby olive groves.

"We gather you've had a bit of a run-in with

the local Greek constabulary, bad luck," Barry commenced.

"Load of jobsworths out to fill their own coffers, it's not as if they don't enjoy the odd tipple on duty," Harold growled. "Six bloody months I've been banned for, six months with no wheels to escape this godforsaken dump. I tell you we have to get out of here; if you've come to make a serious offer on the house you can have it. Joan's threatening to divorce me and go back to England on her lonesome if I don't get a buyer, she can't stand this bloody greasy country."

I caught Barry's eye; things were moving along in his favour much quicker than we'd anticipated.

"But if I come down in price it's on condition of a quick sale, we don't want to be stuck here while you faff about with long drawn-out contracts, we want out as fast as possible. Joan's counting the hours down till we can be back in old Blighty and away from this cat infested dump," Harold continued.

"That suits me, we'd like to move quickly too," Barry said, his knuckles white with tension as he restrained himself from throwing a punch; although a newcomer to Meli, Barry was already a staunch defender of the village.

Having put in a quick call to Spiros to discuss the necessary procedures and legalities of the sale before coming over, I was aware that contracts could be completed in a mere matter of days through the notary and lawyer we had previously used. Since Barry had the cash sitting in the bank there were no pesky hold ups to delay the sale.

"The price will include the carpets and curtains. Will you be wanting the furniture too?" Harold asked.

"No, we'll get new stuff out here, in fact you can take the carpets and curtains as well, best to have the place empty ready for the building work," Barry replied.

My heart sank. Harold hadn't downed enough of the Grouse yet to immune him from taking offence at Barry's words.

"What building work, have you any idea what we've had done to the place? This house needed a heck of a lot of work doing to drag it into the twenty-first century, but now we've knocked it into top-notch shape. Why would you want to go messing with it?" Harold shouted, his unshaven face puce with fury.

"Barry didn't mean to imply it needed major changes, just a few tweaks to keep Cynthia happy," I hastily interjected, relieved to see Harold's temper abate as quickly as it had flared.

"I get you Vic, bloody women, Joan was just the same, had to have that ruddy kitchen imported from England and you wouldn't believe how many colour samples of shag-pile she went through before agreeing with me that purple was perfect. I told her purple all along, but would she listen? Women," Harold scoffed.

"Well it was certainly worth importing the kitchen," I said honestly, acknowledging the kitchen was top quality though in need of disinfecting. "But I think Cynthia's allergic to nylon shag-pile, isn't she Barry, so you might as well ship the carpet back to England with you."

Having caught my drift, Barry improvised, "Nylon shag-pile brings her out in a terrible rash."

"But its best quality nylon," Harold spluttered incredulously, pouring himself another generous measure of Grouse before suggesting, "If the carpet goes you'll be left with nowt but freezing cold tiles."

"I thought you'd ripped all the tiles out when you laid the carpet," I said.

"Only upstairs, the horrible things are still underneath the lounge carpet, see..." Harold invited, walking into the living room and prising a corner of the carpet loose to reveal spectacular mosaic flooring.

"Horrible," Barry cannily agreed. "But at least they won't have Cynthia scratching as though she's bedded down with fleas."

My attention was immediately riveted on the single shelf of books next to the massive flat screen television, though credit must go to Cynthia for the advance warning that Harold was a literary poseur, boasting a collection of classic leather-bound faux books.

"Ah, I see you are a fellow fan of Tobias Smollet," I said, reaching for the imitation copy of Roderick Random.

"Best not to touch it, Joan's only just dusted and fingerprints play havoc on the leather," Harold interjected, steering me firmly away from the bookshelf before I could expose his fake literary pretensions. "Do you want to give the rest of the place another once over, see if there's anything you want leaving before we get down to the brass tacks of money? It seems daft shipping the bed all the way back to England when you'll be needing something to sleep on."

Whilst Harold stepped back on the patio to top up his glass, Barry rolled his eyes at me. I caught his drift; the thought of sleeping in the same bed that Harold and Joan had occupied was too gross to contemplate.

Evaluating upstairs with a critical eye I realised Barry would have his work cut out removing the large picture windows and replacing them with traditional Greek style apertures and wooden shutters. Harold insisted they would leave the curtains; Barry didn't bother to object, whispering to me that they were large enough for him to make use of as dust sheets in his building work. Walking into the bathroom we struggled to maintain our composure at the sight of the soggy shag-pile rising from the floor to frame one side of the gargantuan bath tub.

"You'll easily fit the pair of you in that," Harold chuckled. "There's plenty of room for a good splash, isn't there Joan?"

Addressing Barry directly the blushing Joan interjected, "He means you and Cynthia, not you and Vic." Without another word she hastily tidied the toilet roll away under a grotesque knitted doll sporting a crocheted crinoline in a vibrant orange that clashed with the shag-pile.

"Cynthia will love it," Barry lied. He'd endured enough of his fiancées lectures on the impending world water shortage to know she'd want the tub ripped out and replaced with a shower. If I could only dispel the mental image of Harold and Joan cavorting in the tub I'd be up for persuading Barry to uproot it to my garden. I did miss an occasional soak and an outside bath could be conveniently filled by sticking a hose-pipe onto the hot water tap in the kitchen and angling it out of the window. I pondered if a good going over with Vim would be enough to erase all traces of its former occupants or if the grotesque images would still linger to haunt any luxuriant bubble baths.

"Of course you'll be needing the satellite dish or you'll be stuck with nowt but dismal Greek telly," Harold opined as we stared at the monstrous dish; bracketed to the outside wall it obscured half the view of the village square from the bedroom window. Barry bit his lip rather than respond. Fortunately Spiros was keen to get his hands on the humongous digital receiver to install at his uncle's house as a treat for Sampaguita; she was missing her favourite Filipino television programmes.

Joan was obviously responsible for the bedroom décor; purple satin sheets adorned the bed, festooned with naff matching His and Her embroidered pillow slips. Even the bedside lamps featured gloomy purple tasselled shades. Pressing my fingers against my forehead I attempted to massage away the first pulsating throb of a headache brought on by a violent overdose of purple. For some reason it struck me that the whole bedroom set up had the air of a funeral parlour; the particular hue of the sheets reminding me of the coffin lining when we buried Marigold's Aunty Beryl.

By the time we returned to the patio Harold was conveniently inebriated enough to shake hands on a price that was considerably lower than his initial demands. With the deal shaken on I edged the remainder of the Grouse out of sight, reminding Harold he would need to be up bright, early and sober for our trip to the lawyer's office the next morning.

During my earlier call with Spiros we had arranged to waste no time driving up to town to sign the contract if a price was agreed on, Spiros once again volunteering to guide us through the complexities of Greek bureaucracy. Spiros had drawn the line at letting the despised Harold into the hearse unless he was occupying the back seat coffin, so Barry and I would be stuck with Harold in the Punto, meeting Spiros there.

Chapter 3

Barry's Heartfelt Case of Kefi

The atmosphere was decidedly tense when we returned home, a sullen scowl plastered on Marigold's face as she silently attacked the iron soleplate with a wire scourer. Cynthia, shrouded in guilt, furiously scrubbed away at her orange repping shirt with a washing up sponge, a most unhygienic practice which would necessitate me binning the sponge. Holding the top up to the light revealed the scorched outline of the iron, still clearly visible on the gaudy polyester. Sizing up the situation I advised Marigold to use diluted bicarbonate of soda on the iron and recommended Cynthia bin the shirt as beyond salvageable.

"But I need it for tomorrow's guided tour," Cynthia protested.

"You may borrow mine if you keep it away from the iron," I offered. "If you rinse it out after your shift it will drip dry before I need it for the lazy day cruise."

"Never mind that, how did you get on?" Marigold demanded; her annoyance at the tribulations of sharing a household with her soon to be sister-in-law outweighed by the hope that Barry had secured the property.

"We got it," Barry shouted, picking Cynthia up and swirling her around until she became quite giddy. "Once Harold was oiled up with whisky he agreed to knock down the price."

"Harold's latest run-in with the police was the final straw," I added. "He didn't take much persuasion."

"Plus Joan threatening to return to England without him had rather taken the wind out of his sails," Barry said.

"That's wonderful news," Marigold and Cynthia said in unison, the atmosphere between them visibly lifting now there was light at the end of the house sharing tunnel.

"How soon will you be able to move in?" Marigold asked, making no attempt to mask her eagerness to be rid of Cynthia.

"We're sorting the legalities out tomorrow in town, so we should be out of your hair pretty soon," Barry replied. "Once they move out there's no reason why we can't move straight in. I'm sure we can put up with their execrable décor until it's changed, though we'll probably need access to your bathroom when I get round to fitting a new one."

Before I could claim first dibs on the bathtub Marigold interrupted. "Getting rid of that over-sized bath is a must, it's so tacky. It struck me as the kind of prop that would feature in smutty movies."

"I hardly think Harold and Joan wallowing round in their bathtub would appeal to the dirty mac brigade," I chortled, wondering if my wife's rather bizarre comment had been triggered by a secret perusal of Milton's manuscript.

"I hope you didn't get Harold so sozzled that he'll try to back out when he sobers up," Cynthia said.

"Don't worry, he's desperate to sell. We'll chuck him in the back of the Punto in the morning and deliver him straight to the lawyer's office," Barry assured her.

"I can hardly believe it, we'll be able to start our married life in a place of our very own, Barry," Cynthia gushed.

"Well it will take a while before we get the place as we want it," Barry reminded her.

"Time allowing, you can count on me to help out with any DIY," I offered.

"Thanks Victor," Barry snorted, pointedly not taking me up on my offer.

"This calls for a celebration," Marigold decided.

"The taverna," I suggested.

Arriving at the taverna we stepped inside to exchange greetings with Dina before selecting a table in the outside dining area farthest away from Nikos' barbecue; a necessary precaution to avoid being enveloped in clouds of smoke. Nikos had made little effort to beautify the outside space, the plastic tables and chairs looking as though they'd been randomly discarded on the concrete. Well-thumbed copies of *To Vima* littered the tables alongside empty water bottles Nikos hadn't bothered to bin. Nevertheless the stunning views towards the sea on the horizon captivated our attention and the evening air was heady with the scent of fresh basil plants flourishing in old olive oil tins.

Dislodging a couple of snoozing strays from the chairs, we took our seats. I reflected that things were working out well. With Barry and Cynthia ensconced in their own place before the wedding we wouldn't need to play musical bedrooms when the family arrived from England. Putting up with Harold the next day was a small price to pay to restore domestic harmony, though it would mean delaying my intended visit to the *dimarcheio* to proffer my advice to the mayor on local issues.

Realising how engaged many of my neighbours were with local politics I was determined to add my own voice to the mix, compiling a list of burning issues to bring to the attention of the authorities. I was certain they would be clamouring to capitalise on my wealth of experience, particularly when it came to implementing my ideas regarding innovative sanitary measures for rubbish disposal in the village. The public bins could be a real eye-sore and the fetid stench they disgorged in the summer heat could be assuaged by incorporating a more fastidious approach to disinfecting. Once the mayor familiarised himself with my hygiene credentials he would be sure to realise what an asset I could be. I made a mental note to plump Spiros for insider info on the political leanings of the local council members during our rendezvous in town the next day.

Nikos came over to greet us, grumbling it was too early to light the grill. Dumping a plastic bottle of *spitiko* wine on the table he asked if I wanted to confirm the booking to hold the wedding reception in the taverna. Cynthia fired a 'don't you dare' withering look in my direction, having obviously picked up pointers from Marigold during her stay. Fortunately Nikos was distracted by the arrival of other customers before I could reply. It struck me as odd that the elderly local gents who turned up chose to dine inside the taverna, rather than outside, the stultifying heat inside being quite unbearable at this time of year.

Conversation turned to the choice of venue for the wedding reception. My generous offer to foot the bill for Barry and Cynthia's reception if they held it in the taverna had been graciously received by my brother-in-law, until his intended put her foot down. Since I had no intention of paying for her apparent preference for some version of overpriced fine Greek dining down on the coast, the choice of venue remained unresolved.

"Come on Cyn, you have to make a decision," Barry urged once Nikos was out of earshot. "It makes sense to have the reception in our local and it will be much more convenient for our guests. And we won't get better chips anywhere else."

"I've nothing against having it here, but my parents are flying over for the wedding and mother can be a bit of a snob. She had a fit when I mentioned we were considering a menu of lamb and fried potatoes, saying chips aren't highfalutin enough for a wedding breakfast and she'd rather we went the canapé route," Cynthia said meekly, avoiding my eye. I considered her mother's interference a bit of a cheek since there had been no mention of her footing the bill.

"Did you tell her that Nikos cooks the best food in the Mani and that some of our guests wouldn't know what to do with a canapé?" Barry protested. He made a fair point; even if Panos put on a suit for the wedding he'd still likely pair it with wellies. I could well imagine Kyria Maria's approach to canapés, guzzling anything that took her fancy and dumping anything that didn't appeal back on the platter after a good fingering.

"I doubt any of the restaurants down on the

coast are experienced in preparing canapés, they aren't really a thing over here," Marigold pointed out. The coastal tavernas may be a tad more up-market than our local but they are hardly the Ritz, specialising in good home cooking rather than fancy nouvelle cuisine knocked out by a chef.

"I know, but mother is disappointed enough that I'm not having a big church wedding in England. My parents have never been abroad before and they may disapprove of this place as being a bit spit and sawdust," Cynthia admitted.

"They've never been abroad, that's most unusual these days," I remarked.

"Mother has a morbid fear of flying," Cynthia confessed.

"Well it's your wedding, you must make the decision," Marigold said magnanimously, before adding "but I know that Barry's preference is to hold the reception here and it is his wedding too."

"I'm sure Dina can be persuaded to give the toilet a good scrubbing before the big day and cheer the place up with a bit of bunting and some balloons," I suggested.

"Hmmm, it's just that mother can be a bit of a snob," Cynthia reiterated. "I can just picture her looking down her nose at everything."

"I hope that doesn't include me," Barry joked

whilst Cynthia pointedly avoided his eye. Considering her lack of response a slight, I made a mental note to seat her mother next to Violet Burke at the reception. That should knock any pretension out of her.

Barry's earlier ebullience at securing them a home was in danger of waning as he mulled over the prospect of being stuck with possibly insufferable in-laws. Attempting to cheer Barry up, I advised, "We must make allowances for Cynthia's mother, don't forget she's flying in from the land of keeping up with the Joneses. Not everyone is used to the simple life we appreciate over here."

"You've hit the nail on the head Victor; I love the laidback way of life in Greece," Barry said with heartfelt emotion. Clapping his hands together he successfully splattered a hovering mosquito. "Ever since my first arrival in Meli I've had more appreciation for the simple joys of life. The way the villagers embraced me, accepting me as one of them, was so welcoming."

I reflected how true his words were. Whilst Marigold and I were still attempting to find our feet, Barry was being whisked off his by elderly ladies developing an instant affinity with him. Never had a nasty dose of travel sickness provoked such instant camaraderie between strangers who couldn't speak the same language.

Grabbing Cynthia's hand Barry declared with passion, "Cynthia, our wedding should be a village celebration, not some show that we put on to impress your mother."

"Bravo Barry," Nikos shouted, ambling over with a basket of bread. "You cannot to argue with such the *kefi*."

"*Kefi*?" Cynthia questioned.

"It is, how to say in English, the Greek way of embracing the joy of the life. You are the lucky woman to marry the man with such the *kefi*, life with him will never be the dull," Nikos declared. "You have the wedding party here, we push all the tables together outside, and, I promise you the canape."

"Let's do it," Cynthia relented, a genuine smile on her face.

Leaping up I relieved Eleni of the large bowl of salad, and the olive oil and vinegar she was carrying to our table. With the baby due next month she didn't walk so much as waddle. Burdened by an enormous bump she was obviously uncomfortable in the July heat. Taking a breather she sank into one of the plastic chairs at a nearby table, using an old copy of *Ta Vima* to fan herself vigorously. Wiping the perspiration from her brow she left a visible imprint of smudged newsprint, raising an eyebrow in approval when Barry generously slathered his forearms with vinegar to ward off mosquitoes.

Dina's summer salad was exquisite, the sharp tang of onion perfectly complementing the flavoursome sweet tomatoes, so deliciously ripe we mopped up every last drop of their juices with crusty bread. Nikos tutted in disapproval when he caught me picking the leaves from one of his basil plants, the pungent herb a perfect addition to the salad. It struck him as a strange foreign notion to actually eat the sacred *vasilikos*. As we tucked into succulent chicken wings with salted charred skin, Nikos announced he would be throwing fresh rabbit on the grill the next evening. His words conjured an image of Cynthia's mutant cat chasing Guzim's pet rabbit across my garden and I hoped Doruntina hadn't somehow ended up on the menu. There would be hell to pay if we inadvertently ate Guzim's floppy-eared bed companion.

"I'm afraid we'll have to give the rabbit a miss, it's the monthly meeting of the ex-pat dining club tomorrow," Marigold said. Aware of her reluctance to chow down on bunnies I thought she made a great pretence of looking apologetic as she made our excuses to Nikos.

"Surely it's not time for another get together already," I complained, cringing inwardly at the thought of squandering yet another evening in the enforced company of the dining club, invariably squashed up next to the most tedious man in Meli, Doreen's husband Norman. "It can't be a month since Doreen botched up her evening of fine French dining."

"Doreen knows her French menu didn't exactly go to plan which is why she's insisting on playing hostess again tomorrow," Marigold said.

"I thought the whole idea was to rotate the cooking each month," I objected, thinking it made no sense to give a second chance to Doreen, a woman who obviously considered a tin opener culinary challenging.

"I promised to give her a hand with the cooking," Marigold assured me.

"After blighting the good name of French cooking, which country's delights is she planning to botch this time?" I asked.

"I think she settled on Italian. She was considering serving sushi until I warned her of the dangers of a contagious outbreak of salmonella.

You'll be pleased to note I heard every word when you were droning on about the hazards of sushi," Marigold said, her eyes crinkling with amusement.

"That woman certainly has no business messing about with raw fish, it would only end in disaster," I said, delighted Marigold had heeded my warnings. "Who else has she invited?"

"We couldn't get out of it, Doreen was very insistent. Still I lessened the odds of you being stuck in a cramped corner with Norman by asking Doreen to include Julie and Frank in the numbers," Barry piped up, referencing the two Brits who had purchased a holiday home in the neighbouring village of Nektar. Vangelis and Barry were putting in long days renovating the house and the new owners had flown out for a few days to check up on the progress.

"So there'll be the four of us, Doreen and Norman, and Milton and Edna. I'm looking forward to meeting Julie and Frank," Marigold said, yet to make the acquaintance of the keen cycling enthusiasts.

"Has Doreen invited Spiros?" I asked.

"Victor, it's the ex-pat dining club, Spiros is Greek," Marigold snapped impatiently.

"Yes, but he's dating Sampaguita and she's

an ex-pat, it would be polite to include them," I pointed out, thinking the more the numbers were diluted the less chance I had of being stuck with Norman.

"But she's from the Philippines," Cynthia said. "I think the ex-pat dining club is only open to ex-pats."

"Exactly, Sampaguita is an expatriate from foreign shores. The term, loathsome though I find it, is not limited to foreign residents of British extraction," I argued.

"What do you find so loathsome about the term ex-pat?" Cynthia asked me, looking suitably blank when Barry rudely interjected, "Surely you must have heard Victor's views on this subject."

"It's perfectly ghastly; it conjures up images of Brits like Harold stuffing their faces with all day English breakfasts, swigged down with beer. Personally I regard myself as a European citizen with Greek residency," I explained.

"But I think technically the dining club is limited to ex-pat Brits," Cynthia replied.

"Which is most likely why the evenings are always such a bore, the club needs some new blood. I shall invite Spiros tomorrow, he always livens up any gathering and he wants to introduce Sampaguita to more new people. I feel terrible that I haven't made more effort to meet Sampaguita yet, especially now that she and Spiros are a bit of an item, but busy schedules and all that," I replied.

"It's the decent thing to invite them Victor," Barry said. "Spiros will be a godsend tomorrow steering us through the complexities of Greek bureaucracy, and he does worry that Sampaguita will find life a bit dull being stuck in a small village where most of the residents are pensioned off."

"I wouldn't be at all surprised if she gets bored after the bright lights of Athens. Spiros is quite smitten, but he realises there's more to courting than taking her to church on Sundays," I agreed.

"Sampaguita is delightful company and certainly we must include her in our little gathering," Marigold said hesitantly, a silent 'but' on her lips.

"Spit it out Marigold, what's your reservation," Barry asked.

"I'm just a tad concerned that Sampaguita may insist on hosting the next gathering and serve up fried grasshoppers," Marigold winced.

Barry didn't respond, his attention distracted. Reaching over to Cynthia he ran a hand through her glossy hair. "Hold still a moment, there's something in your hair. Ooh yuck, it's moving."

Patting her head cautiously Cynthia leapt to her feet, shaking her hair vigorously, disturbing a few winged black blobs that dropped onto the paper tablecloth.

"Good gracious, they're everywhere," Marigold cried, dropping her fork in disgust, the square of cheese she had forked suddenly a pulsating black mess. Looking down I noticed the ground was carpeted by a moving mass of insects and I realised we'd been dive-bombed by a colony of flying ants.

"It's a perfectly natural phenomenon," Cynthia said, getting a grip since she'd shaken the insects free from her hair. "It must be the day the ants make their nuptial flight."

"Their nuptial flight?" I queried, mesmerised by a crumb of bread seemingly levitating its way across the table.

"It's an annual flight when the ants look for a new home for their colony, they actually mate in flight," Cynthia explained. Squashing a flying ant between his finger and thumb Barry laughed "at least this one died in the throes of happiness."

"Never mind that, we left the windows open

at home," I shouted, suddenly understanding why the elderly locals had all made a beeline to eat indoors.

Chapter 4

Ripe for a Second Scam

I had an hour to kill before setting off to the lawyer's office in town with Barry and Harold. Armed with a jar of my homemade courgette chutney and a pair of overly plump purple aubergines fresh from the vegetable patch, I called in on Milton and Edna, our impoverished ex-pat village neighbours. Due to their genteel poverty they are always most grateful for any surplus largesse from my garden. I find them to be a most tolerable and thoroughly charming couple, maintaining stiff upper lips despite falling prey to an internet scammer who shamelessly emptied their bank account by exploiting their sympathies for destitute orphans.

The aubergines were rapturously received, Edna commenting that back in England they would undoubtedly sweep first place in a village fete. I couldn't help but notice their rather less enthusiastic reaction to yet another jar of my courgette chutney; I was beginning to regret bottling over one hundred jars of the stuff. Completely chutneyned out, Marigold had banned it from our table, attempting to temper her chutney criticism by saying one could have way too much of a good thing. I must confess to being heartily sick of the stuff too. It is even spurned by the less than fussy kitten notorious for its indiscriminate eating habits, the devil spawn of our imported cat Clawsome and Cynthia's ugly mutant tom. I made a mental note to clear out the cupboard and offer the rest of the chutney to Dimitris to feed his pig.

"I say, these are a pair of glossy beauties old chap," Milton enthused over the aubergines. "I'd grow some myself if the old hip didn't prevent me from grubbing down in the dirt."

"Do come in for a coffee," Edna urged. My heart sank at the thought of Edna's insipid coffee, frugally made with one meagre teaspoon of the cheapest instant rationed between the three of us.

"Perhaps Victor would prefer a cup of Earl Grey," Milton suggested, whispering out of earshot of his wife, "Don't worry, you won't have to share the teabag."

"A cup of Early Grey would be most welcome," I said, crossing my fingers that the teabag wasn't already onto its third dunking.

With Edna busying herself in the kitchen Milton invited me into the living room, confiding, "We've come into a bit of a windfall, we had a stroke of good luck on the old premium bonds, I'd forgotten all about them."

"That's excellent news," I said, genuinely pleased for them.

"Couldn't have come at a better time old chap, it means I can afford to go ahead and get the book published."

Milton's words sent alarm bells ringing; surely it shouldn't cost him anything to publish his porn.

"So you've definitely secured a publisher for your porn?" I queried.

"Erotica old chap, erotica. I took your advice. Edna typed it all up and I sent it off to a literary agent I found on the internet," Milton said.

"And you've had a response so quickly, I was under the impression that sort of thing tended to drag out and involved lots of rejection letters," I said in surprise.

"Well it can do, which is why I decided to invest in the paid services of an agent to read it. You should hear the glowing review she gave 'Delicious Desire', she said it positively pulsated with passion. She practically has me convinced that Scarlett Bottom could be the next Anais Nin, though admittedly the agent hadn't actually heard of the French writer of erotica," Milton said, the merest trace of scepticism apparent in his voice as he considered the agent's literary ignorance.

"Scarlett Bottom?"

"My pen name old chap, you remember you agreed it might put the readers off if they thought an old fogy like me was dabbling in erotica."

"I thought you'd decided to go with Scarlet Richard, Bottom having overtly smutty connotations," I reminded him.

"The agent thought Scarlet Bottom had a more commercial ring to it. It's not entirely inappropriate since she suggested I should make the heroine quite partial to a bit of spanking, though it's not really my cup of tea, and I'd have rather stuck with Richard as my pen name," Milton confided just as Edna returned. Blushing profusely I accepted my cup of tea, the teacup quivering perilously in its saucer as I desperately tried to blank out images of Edna as Milton's muse.

"I don't believe it is customary for literary agents to charge writers to read their work," I cautioned Milton. "Are you sure she is reputable?"

"Well she must be doing okay if she can afford to advertise all over the internet," Milton replied.

"How much did she take you for?" I asked bluntly, almost certain he had been roped in by another scammer.

"I paid one thousand dollars for her expedited reading service, but it was worth every cent as it turns out she's married to the head of a publishing company, stroke of good luck eh," Milton said, his words lacking the conviction his earlier enthusiastic ones had been so full of.

"He might have had to wait months or years to have it read if our premium bond hadn't come up," Edna chimed in.

Hating to put a damper on their dreams I nevertheless decided that brutal honesty was the best policy.

"Let me guess, the publishing company are going to turn your manuscript into book form for a hefty fee..." I ventured.

"As luck would have it they are offering me a twenty percent discount if I can pay by the end of the week," Milton said. "That reduces the price to two thousand dollars for their custom package."

"Their custom package," I repeated, struggling to control the involuntary rise of my eyebrows.

"The agent said the finished custom product would be superior to the basic package," Milton said.

"And what exactly do you get for your two thousand?" I asked.

"They promise a quality paperback with a stunning cover, ten personal author copies, five bookmarks, oh and they include up to twenty-five corrections..." Milton began.

"The corrections are very handy; I might have hit the wrong keys on the typewriter a bit excessively. Milton's words are full of Tippex, my fingers aren't quite as nimble now I have a touch of arthritis in them," Edna interrupted. The gullible pair were apparently clueless it was more customary for manuscripts to go through a rigorous editing process rather than simply be corrected. I could just picture the finished product littered with typos and Tippex, the requisite number of pre-paid corrections stopping abruptly at the end of chapter three. "Don't forget Milton, you get another fifty dollars off the price if you recommend the publisher to a friend."

"It's a pity we can't take advantage of the discount but we don't know anyone else writing a book," Milton sighed; oblivious that I was secretly penning my own book on moving to Greece under the pseudonym of V.D. Bucket, the unfortunate disease riddled name I was stuck with after being abandoned in a bucket at the railway station as a baby. Naturally I would never be so gullible to fall for such an obvious vanity publishing scam and felt it my duty to warn Milton he was being fleeced, even if it did put a spoke in his publishing dreams.

"So you haven't handed any money over yet?" I checked before shattering their dreams.

"Just the reading fee thus far, old chap. I told them I needed to give some thought to going with the custom package rather than the basic, it would clean us out again," Milton said.

"But he'll soon reap it all back in royalties," Edna beamed. "The agent promised it would be a best seller."

"And what is the royalty rate?" I asked.

"Ten percent on every sale if I sign over exclusive rights," Milton replied.

"I really hate to say this Milton but the whole thing stinks of scammers, I believe you have been taken in by a bunch of dodgy crooks preying on writers desperate to see their words in print. It may be too late to recoup the thousand you've already shelled out on the agent, but promise me you won't part with another cent until I can investigate the company for you," I said.

"Oh Victor, tell us what you are thinking, you don't think it's all above board, do you?" Edna pleaded, visibly paling as she exchanged worried glances with her husband.

"I rather suspect you have been targeted and duped by an unscrupulous vanity publishing company. I don't claim to be an expert on the subject, but what I have gleaned from my reading on such matters leads me to believe your erotic manuscript will be turned into a shoddy and overpriced paperback that will never see the light of day in a bookstore," I said. "You would basically be handing over your cash for ten paperback copies of your book, and unless you order additional copies yourself you are unlikely to ever see any royalties."

The realisation that he'd been suckered suddenly dawned on Milton; his posture slumped, his eyes reflecting the knowledge he'd once again been played for a fool. His tone was flat when he rhetorically asked, "You think the promises of 'Delicious Desire' hitting the bestseller lists are lies?"

"I'd put money on it being nothing but spurious hyperbole, and I've never placed a bet in my life," I said. "Not because I have any doubt that your readers would be titillated of course, but because these companies employ salespeople to deliberately target writers rather than actually sell any books."

"Snake oil salesmen from the sound of it. I've been such a gullible fool falling for an unscrupulous press that took advantage of my literary vanity," Milton said in a dejected tone. "It's a rum deal; they'd have fleeced me of the premium bond winnings, but never put my book in front of readers."

"Let me look into the company some more, unfortunately it is a legal con," I offered, reminding him in the meantime to refuse to make any payment no matter how much pressure the con-merchants applied.

"I can't tell you how grateful I am for your sound counsel," Milton said. "What you say makes perfect sense; I was too much of a vain fool to see it. I shall invest in a whistle and blow it down the telephone line next time they phone back pestering me for payment."

"I'm just sorry you've been duped out of a thousand by the fake agent," I said. "Let me look up some reputable ones you can send the manuscript to. Most likely there's a bona fide publishing company that specialises in works of erotica that will be able to give your manuscript the once over. Just promise me you won't be conned into paying, no reputable publisher who wants your book would charge you for the privilege."

"It's a pity you weren't around to stop me being cleaned out by the fake orphans," Milton sighed. "I think the internet should come with a scam warning."

"Plenty of scams predate the internet Milton. I remember reading about thousands of aspiring writers who were conned into parting with their hard earned cash by the Famous Writers School correspondence course back in the 60s before it went bankrupt after being exposed as a scam. It was fronted by some very reputable names in publishing. I don't recall which publishing house he was a big-wig with, but Bennett Cerf said something that stuck in my mind as a cautionary tale, blatantly mocking the people who signed up to the course he was happy to plug."

"What did he say?" Milton asked.

"I believe the exact quote was 'no person of any sophistication, whose book we'd publish, would have to take a mail-order course to learn how to write.'"

I was well versed in the sorry saga. When I began writing my moving abroad book, encouraged by my wife and brother-in-law, Marigold attempted to persuade me to sign up for a correspondence writing course, no doubt convinced they would school me in the art of littering the page with the superfluous exclamation marks she believed to be indispensible punctuation in my chosen genre. Having a natural knack with words I dismissed Marigold's suggestion out of hand, having no intention of taking on any more lessons in addition to Greek ones. Nevertheless I took the precaution of investigating a few scam courses to flaunt in Marigold's face if she should persist in nagging me about their benefits. Cerf's quotation added weight to my assertion that great writers are born, not taught.

"Milton would never have paid for a writing

course, he's a natural, such a way with words," Edna said, her words mirroring my own thoughts about my natural aptitude with words.

"It's just a pity I have such a trusting nature," Milton laughed.

"In my line of work I couldn't afford to take anything on trust; it would likely have resulted in mass outbreaks of food poisoning," I said by way of explaining my tendency to punctiliousness.

"We'll never be able to thank you enough Victor," Edna said. "If you hadn't brought those aubergines round we'd have blown all the premium bond winnings."

"Put it aside for the winter," I advised, happy to know if some other scammer didn't come along to part them from their money they'd at least have some cash stashed away for plenty of cosy log fires. "I'll see you this evening at the expat dining club."

Chapter 5

Faffing About

Scraping the myriad corpses of splattered flying ants from the Punto's windscreen, I cursed Barry's tardiness. He knew we needed to allow ninety minutes for the drive up to town, longer if we were forced to drive around in endless circles looking for a parking space. By the time Barry finally arrived back at the house to leave for our trip to the lawyer's office, he was cutting it fine. Having made a crack of dawn start on the renovation project in Nektar his work clothes were covered in a fine layer of sawdust.

With no time for him to change I took the precaution of covering the passenger seat in a black bin bag before directing the Punto across the village square to collect Harold.

In contrast to Barry's work clothes and my smart shirt, tie and shorts, the vile Brit emerged from his house dressed in dated business garb. The bold blue and white pinstripe suit had clearly seen better days, the jacket straining across his portly stomach, his general appearance leading me to conclude that he'd been in the shady business of flogging second hand cars. On closer inspection it appeared his soberish suit had been donned in an attempt to disguise his obvious hangover. Random scraps of blood stained toilet paper stuck to his jowls and dark glasses concealed his bloodshot eyes.

Climbing into the back of the Punto Harold dispensed with polite greetings. "Hold up a minute, Joan will be along in a tick, she's just putting the finishing touches to her face."

Barry and I exchanged horrified glances, having failed to anticipate that we would be subjected to Joan's cloying presence. With Harold's dismissive attitude towards women we hadn't expected he would drag her along for the business end of things. I squirmed as Joan tripped her way to the Punto in unsuitable high-heeled strappy sandals, her peeling red flesh stuffed into a too tight sundress. Joan had been far too liberal with the cheap scent, necessitating open windows instead of the Punto's air-con. I prayed that the thick layer of makeup coating her face wouldn't drip onto my upholstery once she started sweating in the heat. Taking her cue from her husband, Joan too dispensed with polite greetings, instead moaning, "I hope you can park outside this lawyer chap's office, these shoes are rubbing my blisters something chronic."

"So what's the order of business, the lawyer then a quick bevy?" Harold piped up.

"It's best if we let Spiros set the agenda, it's very good of him to take the time to walk us through the formalities," I replied.

"That bloke always gives me the creeps driving round in that blooming great hearse of his. I like to keep my distance, I bet he stinks of embalming fluid," Harold snorted, Joan breaking into dutiful laughter. Barry and I exchanged a weary glance, knowing we were in for a very long day.

Making our way down to the coast we studiously ignored our back seat passengers. Once we reached sea level Joan demanded that Barry change seats with her, announcing she would likely be overcome with bouts of nausea on the hair-pin bends we were due to approach on the next stretch of the journey.

"If you'd mentioned that yesterday I'd have advised you to come up to town in a taxi. Barry needs to sit in the front as he's prone to travel sickness," I told her, thankful I had a good excuse to avoid Joan's flabby thighs pressing up against my gear stick.

"You should try the local remedy of vinegar and honey," Barry advised smugly. Although pre-armed with a bottle of the disgusting placebo concoction Barry seemed disinclined to share its contents with Joan. No doubt he wished to protect the rim of his bottle from the lurid red lipstick smeared on her teeth.

Weaving through one of the small villages I sighed as we passed a pensioned old gent waving his walking stick, the local method of thumbing a lift. Unfortunately the bulky presence of Harold and Joan meant there was no room for me to play the role of Good Samaritan and I was forced to pass up the opportunity of road-testing my Greek language skills.

"These Greek geriatrics don't half have a nerve expecting free lifts, they're worse than goats for littering the roads," Harold complained.

"So you won't be using that method of getting around then now that you've been banned from driving," Barry retorted. His remark took the wind out of Harold's sails; no doubt he'd been hoping to cadge lifts down to the bars on the coast during his remaining time in Meli, yet considered himself a notch above the elderly Greeks who were too old, rather than too sloshed, to drive.

A herd of goats crossing the road provoked an unscheduled stop. With the car at a standstill the lack of a moving breeze intensified the heat to an unbearable degree, even though it was still well before noon. Despite my misgivings about breathing in recirculated air I was tempted to close the windows and turn on the air-con until I caught sight of Joan's greenish hue in the rear view mirror. I decided it would be more prudent to advise her to stick her head out of the open window for the rest of the journey.

"It wouldn't be so bad if you didn't drive like a maniac," she whined. "There's no need to take the bends as though you're at Brands Hatch."

"I'll try to go at a more sedate pace," I told her, accelerating past the goats, realising I had indeed been driving at a speed in excess of my more usual sedate pace, desperate to arrive at our destination and escape the sickly smell of Joan's nasty cheap perfume.

"You can always get a taxi back when we've finished in town," Barry suggested.

"What, and pay those rip-off prices? A double brandy will fix Joan up nicely before we head back, I told her she should have had a snifter with breakfast to settle her stomach," Harold responded.

"I haven't got time to waste sitting round in bars," Barry objected. "Some of us have work to get back to."

"But surely you'll want to celebrate buying our house," Harold said.

"There'll be time for that when you've packed up and moved out," Barry assured him.

Apart from Harold emitting the odd strangled snore, our back seat passengers remained silent for the remainder of the journey. Harold floundered out of his hung-over snooze when I pulled into a petrol station on the outskirts of town for a top up of unleaded. Surprisingly Harold had something complimentary to say about Greece, admitting he would miss the cheap petrol prices and the convenience of having a forecourt attendant fill the tank rather than having to do it himself.

"But you won't need to do it at all now that you've been banned from driving," Barry smugly reminded him.

"I've only been banned in Greece, I hardly think the Greeks are so competent that they'll have announced it to the boys in blue back home," Harold retorted, seemingly oblivious that his driving licence would bear an international blemish. Considering we wanted to keep Harold on side until his signature was on the house sale contract, Barry and I prudently made no comment.

"I can't get over the brilliant free service these places offer over here," Barry observed as the attendant made a sterling job of removing the last trace of splattered ants from the windscreen.

"Excellent indeed. I'll just get him to check the air in the tyres then we can be on our way," I replied, paying for the petrol without exiting the driver's seat.

Spiros' hearse, illegally parked half on the pavement outside the lawyer's office, was a welcome sight when we arrived. Even though the lawyer Spiros had engaged spoke impeccable English, it was a relief for Barry to have the undertaker along in his role as self-appointed sponsor, to guide him through the complexities of Greek bureaucracy. Harold and Joan shuffled impatiently as the lawyer exchanged polite greetings with me, recalling our previous dealings over the house purchase in Meli. Harold and Joan became even tetchier when he greeted Barry with similar enthusiasm, delighted to hear he was related.

Harold brusquely cut the lawyer short when Spiros introduced them, demanding we get straight down to business without all this "unnecessary faffing about." Looking suitably confused the lawyer asked "what is the faffing?" Harold tutted rudely as Spiros apparently translated the phrase into Greek, saying *"ton agnoei, einai ena kefali poutinkas."* Attempting to suppress a wry smile, the lawyer's eyes twinkled. I recognised that Spiros had told the lawyer to ignore Harold, but it was Barry who whispered the rest of the translated sentence to me, his effort to learn builder's Greek having apparently encompassed the insulting term 'pudding-head'. Naturally the disparaging label went over Harold's head; he hadn't wasted a single moment of his four-year sojourn in Greece on bothering to learn even one word of the language.

Amazingly Harold was able to proffer a neatly bound file containing all the documents pertaining to his original house purchase and the building work he'd commissioned on the property. The lawyer perused the contract with a fine tooth comb, stating everything was in order, apart from the matter of the swimming pool which Harold had failed to declare to the tax authorities.

"This must to be declared, the authorities are clamping down on the illegal pools," the lawyer advised.

"Oh, there's no worries there," Harold blustered. "I have a huge green plastic cover. Every time a helicopter flies over I dash out and cover the pool to keep it out of sight of prying eyes. From helicopter height it must look just like another green splodge of olive grove."

Spiros rolled his eyes at this revelation, no doubt amused that Harold was clueless the recent bout of helicopters had been swooping up seawater to dump on forest fires.

"We'll be getting rid of the swimming pool," Barry piped up. "It's a ridiculous luxury in a village with a precarious water supply."

"Are you off your trolley?" Harold shouted. "It's the finest pool for miles; you'll be the envy of all the other ex-pats with a pool as grand as that. It will give you boasting rights and impress all the plebs."

"I have no intention of incurring the unnecessary expense of maintaining a pool, and anyway Cynthia is determined to turn it into an ecological pond," Barry insisted.

"A what?" Harold and Joan questioned in unison.

"An ecological pond, an environmentally friendly natural habitat for birds and flying insects to breed and flourish, whilst increasing local biodiversity," Barry explained.

"So you plan to get rid of our pool and replace it with a pond, what and fill it with frogs?" Harold asked, clearly baffled.

"Frogs, dragonflies, water stick insects, likely bats too," Barry confirmed.

"You're bleeding mad," Harold scoffed.

After a final perusal of the contract the lawyer proclaimed everything was in tip-top order to proceed with the sale. Fortunately Barry had already taken care of acquiring a Greek tax number and numerous photocopies of his passport when he'd arrived in Greece the previous month.

With the price settled on the previous evening we had presumed this aspect of the sale would be straightforward, but Harold immediately demanded that a significant cash bump be exchanged under the table. Barry was happy to go along with this since Spiros had explained to him that only the objective value of the house needed to be declared on paper. The lawyer confirmed this was perfectly standard practice and Barry's purchase tax liability would be significantly reduced if he was paying less on paper than the actual amount that would be handed over. However Harold complicated matters by demanding a higher cash percentage than the lawyer could legitimately get away with concealing. After launching a fruitless bartering exercise Harold finally saw reason, agreeing to the cash amount the lawyer had originally proposed, satisfied by the legal explanation that had he declared the reduced objective value of the house since he'd purchased it, it would likely attract the unwanted attention of the tax man.

Barry sighed in relief that he could now move on to signing the first ream of paperwork, only to be frustrated when Joan stuck her two penn'orth worth in, questioning why the paper value of the house had hardly increased a cent during the last four years despite the small fortune they'd shelled out on home improvements. Fortunately her interference was short lived when Harold snapped "Give it a bloody rest woman; it's sorted with a cash bung."

There was one more hurdle to overcome before Barry could sign on the dotted line on the preliminary contract, agreement on a completion date. With the wedding in less than two weeks Barry was obviously keen to move into the house before the big day. With the way Harold and Joan complained endlessly about living in Greece it had seemed to be a no-brainer that they would wish to flit at the first opportunity, yet Joan immediately threw a spanner in the works, announcing that the completion date Barry proposed was quite impossible. "It will take us at least a month to pack everything up; we're not exactly short of worldly belongings you know."

"I thought you wanted to be on your way back to England as soon as possible," Barry argued.

"Well of course we do, but you can't expect us to just cram everything into a couple of duffel bags and be on our way. We've even more to pack than we had when we moved out here four years ago," Harold said.

"I'm sure a removal firm could help you to speed things along," I politely suggested, attempting to hide my exasperation that the pair of them had spent the last four years accumulating so much excess junk and clutter that packing it up could hinder Cynthia's departure from my home.

"I owned a removal company back in Manchester, we employed very experienced packers, they can box up a whole house the size of yours in less than eight hours," Barry said.

"I don't want some strange fellows rifling through my things, I want to pack properly," Joan argued, her voice rising to a fever pitch when she added, "We have a lot of valuables to consider."

"You'll save a lot of time by binning all those bikinis, you won't have much call for them in England, not to mention budgie smugglers are well out of fashion," Barry snapped.

"Oh Harold, I don't know how we'll manage without a pool, I feel like we'll be slumming it," Joan wailed.

Barry and I exchanged a worried glance, realising we needed to get Harold to sign on the dotted line before Joan succumbed to sudden nostalgia for their flashy swimming pool and decided she wanted to stay in Greece.

"I'll get you one of them heated hot tubs in the garden, it'll make all the new neighbours green," Harold assured his wife.

"So the completion date? Shall we say the 27th," Barry hurriedly suggested, citing the date the family were due to fly over from England. The date was perfect since it would free up the spare bedroom, currently occupied by Barry and Cynthia, for Violet Burke.

"That's impossible, I can't possibly get everything packed up in less than a week," Joan said firmly.

"Look, you're keen to get in and we're keen to get out. How about we say the last day of the month?" Harold countered.

"Even that's pushing it, you'll have to help me with the packing Harold," Joan complained.

"I'll take it," Barry said. "Let's shake on the last day of the month."

Desperate to secure a speedy completion date my brother-in-law appeared to have overlooked the date that Harold had chosen was his wedding day.

Pen poised in hand, the lawyer prepared to ink the completion date onto the contract. Just then his telephone rang.

Chapter 6

Cheese Pies All Round

Answering the phone, the lawyer gestured that we should take five minutes whilst he embarked on a telephone consultation. Spiros wasted no time in seizing the opportunity to escape outside for a crafty cigarette, Barry and I wasting no time in following him.

"I thought Harold was going to back out when his stupid wife started chuntering on about missing the pool," Barry said, bumming a cigarette from Spiros even though he doesn't smoke.

"Is that why you agreed to the thirty-first?" I

asked.

"Had to get a date sorted, I'm a bag of nerves dealing with that windbag," Barry replied, greedily inhaling the nicotine before succumbing to a bout of coughing. Tossing the half-smoked cigarette aside and grinding it out with his heel, he added, "Cynthia's going to be chuffed that we can move in after the wedding rather than honeymooning in your spare room."

"I honestly thought that you'd forgotten the completion date clashes with your wedding," I said, thinking this was perhaps not the best moment to break the news that he and Cynthia would need to turn the spare room over to my mother when she flew in. There would be no arguing with Violet Burke; she was prone to tyrannical tendencies.

"Don't be daft, the date is etched on my brain. Sorry we'll be cluttering your place up in the run up to the wedding Victor, I'd suggest staying in a hotel if it wasn't for all the extra expense buying the house will entail. I've just realised you'll likely need your spare room back when your guests arrive. I'll bed down on the sofa and Cynthia can squeeze in with Violet Burke so the boys can have your office," Barry offered. "We've already decided to postpone the actual honeymoon because of the move, there's no point Cynthia turning down summer work when it's thin on the ground in winter."

"Well the important thing is that once you sign you'll be in your new place by the end of the month," I said, wondering how he imagined he could persuade Cynthia to share a bed with my mother. They hadn't exactly hit if off on her last visit.

"I am the happy you have found the house," Spiros said to Barry. "It is the pity I not to have one in the village to sell you. Tell me Barry, how is the house of the dead uncle in the Nektar coming along in the building work?"

"Very well, Frank and Julie were over yesterday, they were delighted with the progress," Barry said.

"Ah, I must to make the time to meet with them again," Spiros said.

"They'll be at the meeting of the ex-pat dining club this evening, we were hoping you and Sampaguita could join us," I invited.

"What is the ex-pat dining club Victor?" Spiros asked.

"It's just a gathering of friends meeting to eat home cooked foreign food. It was set up as an experimental foray into the cuisines of different cultures. We'll be meeting at Doreen's house this evening," I explained.

"And the Doreen will to cook the alien food? Is it the foreign food like the curry you cook?" Spiros said. His features contorting in disgust reminded me he wasn't a big fan of the chicken curry I'd knocked up in the slow-cooker.

"I think she's cooking Italian."

"Ah, that is the good. You know the most famous Italian food, the *pitsa*, was invented in the Greece?"

Barry attempted to stifle a snort but I rushed to assure him that Spiros wasn't actually spouting mere patriotic nonsense. "It's true Barry, the ancient Greeks first came up with the concept of pizza, cooking up *plakous* in a primitive mud oven."

"*Plakous*?" Barry queried.

"A flat bread with herby toppings," I explained.

"So the Greek word for pizza is *plakous* then?"

"No, it's *pitsa*. Modern Greek has moved on from the ancient tongue."

"So the Doreen is cooking the *pitsa*? I think the Sampaguita enjoy very much the *pitsa*," Spiros said.

"I've no idea what Italian dish she'll be concocting, but I wouldn't bank on it being pizza since it doesn't come out of a tin," I said. "Still it will be a good opportunity for you to introduce Sampaguita to some new people; I for one am very much looking forward to meeting her, I can't believe our paths haven't crossed yet. She may feel a bit cut off stuck in the house caring for your old and sickly uncle, a night out will do her good."

"It is true the unhealthy uncle is not the best of the company. I will bring Sampaguita to your, what was it again Victor?"

"The ex-pat dining club." The words were no sooner out of my mouth than Harold and Joan sidled up next to us on the pavement looking most put out, having overheard talk of a club they were pointedly excluded from.

"I'm surprised at you going along to that club Vic, I was under the impression you thought you were better than the rest of us ex-pats," Joan said.

"And I've heard you like to slum it in that dump of a local where you suck up to the bleeding Greeks," Harold sneered.

"I wouldn't concern yourself about where I choose to socialise Harold, we obviously move in different circles," I replied, determined not to rise to the bait. Barry put a restraining hand on Spiros' shoulder before he could make a move that would be unbecoming for a local undertaker.

"We find there's an altogether better class of company down on the coast, don't we Harold, not half as stuffy or stuck-up as that lot in Meli," Joan piped up, clearly miffed they hadn't been invited to make up the numbers that evening.

Changing the subject Harold said, "Bloody rude of that lawyer chap to take that call when we need to finish up so we can get to the bank. No concept of time, these Greeks."

"It's always the same in this country, you make the effort to turn up in person, but the person who phones in gets all the attention," Joan complained.

"Well he did rearrange his diary to squeeze us in on short notice," I reminded her.

"I'm sure he'll rip us off in inflated charges for his services," Harold snapped peevishly just as the door opened and the lawyer beckoned us to return inside.

I exhaled in relief when Harold and Barry added their monikers to the dotted line, confirming the property would be transferred to Barry on his wedding day. With the formalities out of the way a pleasantly plump middle-aged woman put in an appearance, bearing a tray of biscuits and six tiny cups of Greek coffee, the lawyer introducing her as his wife.

Only Spiros welcomed the appearance of coffee which would inevitably delay our departure, the rest of us having no wish to drag out the encounter or make small talk amongst ourselves. Barry and I sipped our coffee politely whilst Harold rudely rejected his, muttering it was a pity the lawyer couldn't offer something stronger.

"I don't mind if I do," Joan said enthusiastically, stuffing a handful of biscuits in her mouth.

"*Einai nostima,*" I said to the lawyer's wife, appreciatively declaring the *kourabiedes* delicious as I took a bite.

"*Tous ekana fresco simera to proi.*" Her smile didn't fool me. Her declaration that they were fresh from her oven that morning was a blatant lie; I immediately recognised the cookies as the same shop bought brand of almond biscuits Marigold deluded herself were home baked.

Fortunately our business with the lawyer concluded on a good note when after checking his diary he mentioned he would have business in our area with the notary *methavrio*, and Barry and Harold could meet him there for the notary's

72

reading and final signing of the contract. Barry and I exchanged relieved glances that we would be spared another trip up to town in the company of Harold. Even with Spiros in tow, Barry appreciated my presence, relying on my sound counsel in my role of older brother-in-law.

There was still the bank to attend to before our business with Harold could be concluded, since Harold was desperate to get his grubby hands on the ten percent cash deposit, a sum he would forfeit if he backed out of the sale before signing the final contract. After telling me he was sure I could manage the bank without his help, Spiros elected to sit it out in a coffee shop close enough to the bank for me to drag him out if my Greek language skills weren't up to assisting Barry with the monetary transaction.

Putting my foot down I whisked us from the lawyer's office to the bank, conscious it was nearing closing time. Harold kept up a running complaint that he had never been shown any respect by the bank staff, even though he had thousands stashed in his account. Imagining Harold expected to be treated with an air of entitlement he wasn't due, I didn't respond. After parking the Punto we legged it to the bank, Joan trailing behind at a distance, complaining her high-heeled shoes weren't designed for speed-walking. Having never visited the bank so near to closing time before, I was pleasantly surprised to find just a trickle of customers instead of the usual unruly mob. Grabbing a ticket I made a mental note to arrive at a similar time in future rather than earlier, adding it to my store of knowledge about Greek banking habits which included always avoiding the bank on pension pay-out day.

The rather unkempt and casually dressed bank manager, working at his usual desk surrounded by the ubiquitous haze of cigarette smoke, leapt to his feet, rushing to double kiss me on both cheeks and ask after Marigold. The double kiss was a new development in our relationship and I noted Barry must still be considered a bit lower in the pecking order as he only received a handshake.

The bank manager was delighted we'd called in as he was able to personally present Barry with his cash machine card. It appeared the bank was finally making efforts to move into the twenty-first century; it was only three weeks since the card had been ordered. When I mentioned that we hadn't seen him in the local taverna lately he made his excuses, saying he only frequented the place in winter, having been driven away by a plague of flying ants on the last occasion he'd eaten there in summer. Harold shuffled impatiently behind us, clueless the scruffy smoker was in charge of the branch.

Our conversation was cut short when Barry's ticket came up and we moved to the cashier's window to withdraw the deposit. Within minutes of requesting the cash a neat stack of fifty euro notes whizzed through a modern electronic note counter before being shoved into Barry's hands. Barry was clearly taken aback by the speed of the transaction, commenting how favourably it contrasted to the painfully slow process of withdrawing a much smaller amount from his building society account back in England after giving the requisite seven days' notice. Since such a large sum of cash made Barry uneasy, he was happy to hand the notes over to Harold.

"I'm glad I don't have to carry such a large sum around," Barry confided in me. "I'd have felt a bit self-conscious trying to stuff all those notes into the security pocket Marigold insisted on sewing into my underpants."

Cracking his knuckles and beaming broadly, Harold threw a sociable arm around Barry's shoulders, insisting, "Come on, let's find a bar, the drinks are on me." He was like a different person now that he had a wad of cash stuffed in his back pocket, no trace of his former rancour evident as he grinned jovially.

"It's the middle of the day and I've got work to get back to," Barry declined.

"And I'm driving," I added.

"But it's not every day we get to celebrate going back to old Blighty," Harold insisted. "Come on, just one for the road, Joan can't face the drive back without a brandy to settle her stomach."

"Well we do need to catch up with Spiros, no doubt we'll find him knee deep in cheese pies and coffee," I relented.

"That's the ticket, the cheese pies are on me," Harold said.

"Blimey, what's he done with the old Harold," Barry hissed in my ear. "Perhaps we should invite them along this evening as a gesture of goodwill."

"Let's not be too hasty," I cautiously advised. "We've still got to get them back to Meli."

"You manage the good?" Spiros asked as we joined him at an outside table in the shade of a leafy pear tree.

"All sorted thanks," Barry assured him as Harold waylaid a waiter, placing an order for double Metaxas for him and Joan, coffees for Spiros, me and Barry, and cheese pies all round. Even though it was evident that Spiros had already eaten by the flaky detritus of pie surrounding him, he didn't decline another one and he'd never been known to say no to coffee even when already awash with the strong beverage. With the order placed Harold and Joan disappeared inside to locate the toilets whilst Barry and I caught up with Spiros.

"I telephone to the Sampaguita. My fragrant Filipana flower will come to eat the *pitsa* on this evening," Spiros announced, brushing a mess of pie crumbs to one side. "She is the little, how you to say, shy."

"She'll be fine, we're a very welcoming bunch," I assured him, making a mental note to make sure that Sampaguita wasn't stuck in a dark corner with that boring splodge of porridge, Norman. "I take it the romance is going well."

"Sampaguita has steal my heart, she fill me with the *romantikos* feel," Spiros declared, licking some flaky cheese pie crumbs from his fingers.

"And does she reciprocate your feelings?" Barry asked.

"*Ti?*"

"Reciprocate," I repeated, thumbing through

my handy English to Greek dictionary. "Ah, here we are; *antapodido*."

"She say to me 'Spiro, you are my handsome Greek god' and when the Kyria Booras drop down from the heart disaster..." Spiros paused to make the sign of the cross, "the Sampaguita come to the help, she tweezer the hairs from the Kyria Booras' chin with the gentle touch before I display the body in the coffin."

"It must be love," Barry muttered, raising his eyebrows when Spiros blushed.

"Many, many the woman feel the revulsion for my business with the dead bodies. The wife say the reason she divorce me is I always bring to the bed the smell of the embalming fluid. But the Sampaguita is the different, she care very much for the corpse and appreciate the ritual of the dead. The Sampaguita comb the hair of the dead Sotiris Sfetsas with the tenderness I could not to imagine, she steal my heart, not one the person could stand the *dysarestos malaka* but the Sampaguita give the respect," Spiros said with heartfelt passion, furtively wiping a lone tear from his cheek. Spiros' emotion touched us as he recalled the tenderness with which Sampaguita handled the corpse of a thoroughly unpleasant local who even in death deserved Spiros' unrepeatable profanity.

"It sounds as though you should snap her up Spiro," Barry encouraged. "I wonder if Cynthia would go for a double wedding."

"First I must to the propose," Spiros said, his broad wink not quite belying his serious tone.

Chapter 7

Not Quite a Flop

It was late afternoon by the time I reached home following the trip to town. The house was blissfully quiet. I discovered Marigold asleep in the bedroom with Clawsome and Catastrophe curled up on the pillow beside her, *my* pillow I noted in horror, cat fur imperceptibly being shed in the breeze from the fan. An open notebook laid face down beside Marigold, her fingers still clasped a pen I gently removed from her grasp. She'd been doing a lot of furtive scribbling recently, but remained adamant it was none of my business. Closing the notebook I moved it to the bedside table, respecting her privacy by squashing the natural urge to sneak a peek inside, dismissing the absurd notion that Marigold may be penning her own exclamation mark littered account of our move to foreign shores.

Thoughts of my book brought me up short. I really did need to get on with writing the Bucket saga, having failed to pen a single word since introducing the Albanian shed dweller to potential readers. Speaking to Milton earlier put me to shame; he'd actually been assiduous in putting words on the page rather than prevaricating. Still, I reasoned, it wasn't as though Milton exactly had much else going on his life, whilst I had the encumbrance of a part-time job as a tour guide, not to mention a brood of chickens to endure.

I wondered how long Marigold had been dozing. She'd taken to enjoying a siesta as soon as the summer temperatures soared, but it was a habit I found I just couldn't acclimatise to. There had been no siestaing on the job during my illustrious career as a public health inspector, though I suspected Marigold and Geraldine may have occasionally enjoyed post pet food tasting naps in their staff room, after occasionally over indulging in a new brand of puppy formula.

"How long have you been home?" my wife asked sleepily, rubbing her eyes.

"I just got back. I was hoping I could persuade you to join me for a stroll. We could get a head start warding off all the calories we'll be consuming this evening."

"Just give me a minute to rinse my face and I'll be right with you," Marigold said, stretching languidly. "It's a tad hot for walking though, why don't we make it a swim instead. I'll drive, since you've been stuck behind the wheel most of the day."

"A swim sounds wonderful," I impetuously agreed.

Driving down to the coast I filled Marigold in on the events of the day whilst drinking in the spectacular views, appreciating how the light changed with the passing of seasons.

"As much as I love Barry, I had hoped he and Cynthia would be out of our hair before the boys arrive," she said. "It's going to be a dreadful squash with seven of us and only the one bathroom."

"It's only for a couple of days, we should be able to manage unless there's an issue with the water supply. Barry and Cynthia will be moving into Harold's house on their wedding day."

"So it all went smoothly, no hiccups? You managed to get Harold back to Meli without killing him," Marigold asked jokingly.

"Well funnily enough we left him and Joan down on the coast..."

"You mean you had to put up with his ghastly wife too? Thank goodness I used Doreen's need for kitchen assistance as an excuse not to come along."

"Unfortunately we had to put up with Joan. Still, they weren't too bad on the drive back, they mellowed considerably once they had their hands on Barry's deposit. When we got back to the coast they asked me to drop them off, they wanted to celebrate in the bar they frequent and said they'd make their own way back up to Meli later," I said.

The village I'd dropped them in was the same village we were heading to for our late afternoon swim. Marigold immediately suggested a change of swimming venue, worried that we may run into Harold and Joan. The bar they frequented was close to our favourite beach spot and Marigold was concerned that our paths may cross and we'd end up ferrying the two drunks back with us later.

"I know how much you fancy trying out the diving board," Marigold teased, suggesting we head to a nearby coastal spot with a diving platform instead of beach access to the water. An uneasy recollection flooded over me. Several weeks earlier I'd imbibed a little too much of Nikos' *spitiko* in the taverna; under the influence I had boasted about the diving prowess of my youth, recklessly saying I was up for giving it another whirl. Surely my wife could tell I was being flippant since I hadn't actually tottered on the edge of a diving board since my school-boy days in the local swimming baths.

"Of course I'm up for it, but it won't be any fun for you being deprived of a swim," I countered with a bluff, knowing full well that Marigold would never launch herself into the sea from a great height.

"But I won't miss my swim Victor, Athena told me there is a convenient ladder leading from the diving platform into the sea," Marigold replied.

"Really," I muttered, cursing Athena and her big mouth. "But surely you'd prefer to ease into the water gradually from solid sandy ground, rather than grapple with a wet ladder."

"Athena says it's a perfectly sturdy ladder, it

will be fine, it's not as though I inherited Barry's vertigo," Marigold said. Refusing to hear another word on the matter she speeded up towards our destination, a tinkling laugh escaping her lips at the thought of the precarious position my tipsy boasting had landed me in.

The diving platform was sited some distance away from the centre of the small fishing village which was our destination, off to one side of the picturesque harbour filled with colourful fishing boats bobbing at anchor. Driving through the village Marigold slowed down, our progress impeded by sunburned tourists ambling in the road, mindless of traffic as they perused menus and took photographs of the traditional quaint setting. Our route took us past the bustling harbour, local fisherman relaxing in the harbour-side taverna, newly awakened from their daily siesta. A smattering of different languages reached my ears, English mingling with German, Swedish, and the occasional American accent.

Despite the lack of a beach, the platform appeared to be a popular spot for local children. There were at least half-a-dozen of them vying for a spot on the diving board or splashing around in the water at the base of the ladder, waiting their turn to climb back up out of the sea for another dive. The children had obviously been brought up with impeccable manners towards their elders; politely treading water they indicated Marigold should make her way down the ladder before they ascended.

"I'll see you in the water," Marigold said, tentatively grasping hold of the rungs as she made her way down the ladder, whilst I hovered to one side, my stomach lurching into my mouth at the thought of venturing out onto the diving board. It looked like an awfully long drop down, the calmness of the water doing little to quell my stomach churning apprehension.

Two Greek boys aged about ten years old jostled each other, playfully fighting for the next spot on the diving board. Spotting my awkward stance one of the boys demonstrated his exemplary manners, pushing his friend out of the way as he called out "*parakalo prochoriste*," inviting me to go next.

"*Ochi, meta apo sas*," I replied; no, after you.

The boys didn't need telling twice. The one who had spoken stepped confidently out on the board, executing a perfect dive into the water. Not to be outdone his friend quickly followed, showing off with an impressive backward somersault.

"Come on Victor," Marigold shouted, waving at me from the water.

Clammy fear took hold of me as I contemplated doing something a couple of ten year olds had managed so gracefully. Casting my mind back to my own childhood days I remembered the confidence I'd felt when I'd dived fearlessly into the pool, but it seemed to have deserted me now. I was still dithering when the two boys who'd dived made their way over the top of the ladder, eager for another go. Shuffling to one side I repeated my invitation for them to go first, reassessing my hasty assumption that they were well mannered when the pair of them taunted me insultingly, shouting, "*kotopoulo.*"

Being publicly called out as a chicken by a pair of loud-mouthed louts was too much; shouldering the death-or-glory spirit of intrepid Greek heroes I stepped boldly onto the diving board, making it to the very edge before my bravado wavered. The next thing I knew I was floundering towards the sea, rudely helped on my way by a vigorous shove from the ghastly young oiks who had crept up behind me. I barely had time to keep a firm grip on my swimming shorts and hold my nose before I landed with a splat in the water, splashing seawater all over Marigold's head.

"Victor, you could be more careful," Marigold complained, "you know I don't like to get my hair wet."

"You should swim in a hat then," I retorted after coughing up the sea water I'd swallowed, pointing out the three Greek grannies treading water nearby, all kitted out in wide brimmed sun-hats. Wondering if they were connected to the boys who had unceremoniously pushed me in, I considered giving them a piece of my mind.

"That wasn't much of a dive, are you going to give it another go?" Marigold asked.

"No, I think I'll just stay in the water, it's most relaxing."

"At least you didn't do a belly flop. Imagine how the children would have made fun of you if you'd flopped."

Chapter 8

Searching for the Senior Escapee

We were just leaving the house for the monthly meeting of the ex-pat dining club when Spiros telephoned, urgently requesting my help with a personal emergency. Considering the amount of times Spiros had so generously helped me out I didn't hesitate for a moment, the least I could do was dash to his assistance.

"But we'll be late for Doreen," Marigold remonstrated. "She's cooking chicken parmesan and it will end up all rubbery if we're late."

"Better rubbery than raw," I said, always suspicious of amateurs let loose on poultry. I wondered what had possessed a culinary numpty like Doreen to think she could handle such a complicated dish involving breading, frying and baking; no doubt she had binge watched an episode too many of 'MasterChef', though her botched Peking duck had proved a recipe for disaster more reminiscent of 'Kitchen Nightmares'.

"You and Cynthia go along and make our apologies, we'll follow you over as soon as we've helped out Spiros," Barry said, not hesitating in joining forces with me to help Spiros out with his personal emergency.

Five minutes later we met up with Spiros in the village square. As Spiros was smartly dressed in a suit and tie, the garb he wore in his official capacity as village undertaker, our immediate instinct was to hope the emergency wasn't coffin related. Dealing with a cadaver would definitely quell our appetite for pasty complexioned chicken.

Spiros appeared quite overwrought, out of breath and frantically running his fingers through what was left of his hair. He had called in at the barber's in town earlier, always eager to impress a date with a touch of personal grooming that avoided the lopsided neckline guaranteed by Apostolos, the local barber.

"Victor, Barry, you are the good friends to come. I need the help to find the uncle, he is the nowhere to be found. When the Sampaguita go to put on the dress for the *pitsa* evening, the uncle escape the house."

"He escaped!" Barry exclaimed, exchanging confused glances with me. We hadn't realised that Spiros' uncle was held captive against his will.

"We have lost the Uncle Leontiades; he is the too old and infirm to be out on the own, it is not the safe for him now his mind is, how you say, going down the toilet."

"Down the pan," Barry corrected.

"We're with you Spiro, it sounds as though your uncle perhaps has a touch of dementia. It must be very worrying if he's wandered off," I sympathised.

"Terrible," Barry agreed. "Victor, you remember what a run-around old Aunty Beryl gave us when she started to lose her marbles?"

"I'll never forget the winter morning she went gallivanting off, managing to get all the way to Hollingsworth Lake by sneaking onto the back of a milk float," I recalled with a shudder. It had taken the three of us the best part of a Saturday morning to locate Aunty Beryl. Since she wasn't quite with it, to put it politely, it proved impossible to convince the life-long spinster that she wasn't actually married to the milkman. To his credit he continued to leave a pint on Aunty Beryl's doorstep every morning, even though his wife divorced him, convinced he'd been carrying on with Aunty Beryl for years; her beauty was still quite striking, if somewhat faded.

"It's a wonder she didn't freeze to death in nothing but that winceyette nightie," Barry said, reminding me there had been snow on the ground.

"We might never have found her if we hadn't followed the milk float's tracks in the snow. At least we don't need to worry about Spiros' uncle freezing," I said, already beginning to sweat in the heat. I wondered if it would be too risky to ditch the socks I paired with my sandals. The sweaty wool was beginning to irritate my skin, but my naked ankles would be too much of a sweet temptation for blood sucking mosquitoes.

"The uncle is the used to the air conditioning, he will to find the heat very tiring," Spiros said.

"Well at least we don't have to worry about him running off with the milkman since Meli doesn't have one," Barry joked.

Sensing from Spiros' worried scowl that he was in no mood for frivolous quips, I suggested we formulate a plan of action to find Leontiades. Spiros told us he had the home base covered. Sampaguita was waiting at the house and would telephone his mobile if the wanderer returned. Meanwhile Vangelis and Panos were out trawling one end of the village, and the three of us would scour the other end.

"It might help if we knew what he looked like," Barry pointed out since neither of us had met the reclusive old gent.

"The uncle is the small man with the white head and the proud moustache," Spiros said, helpfully adding, "The Sampaguita say he go out without the dress."

"Well a naked man should be pretty easy to spot," I said.

"He is not the naked, he wear the dress for the bed," Spiros clarified. Fortunately Barry and I were accustomed to the Greek habit of referring to clothes as dresses so we instantly realised we were searching for a small elderly infirm man wearing pyjamas, rather than a winceyette nightie like Aunty Beryl.

"I'll check the church out, why don't you two

ask if anyone's seen him in the shop," Barry suggested.

Unfortunately Tina who ran the village shop was nowhere to be seen, having left her stroppy mother Despina to man the store. Despina was a brusque woman with an unpleasant disposition from a neighbouring village whose husband had recently absconded with another woman. She now spent a lot of the time ostensibly helping her daughter in the shop; in reality she was nothing but a hindrance to the business, wearing her abandonment as an excuse to treat every male customer with undisguised contempt, her censorious glares blaming every man who stepped through the door of sharing responsibility for her jilted state.

She had the disturbing habit of accusing the male customers of ogling her with lecherous intent, seemingly oblivious they were transfixed by the bulbous and hairy wart positioned directly between her eyebrows. Despina's features reflected her jaundiced view, her visage bearing a distinctly yellowish hue which reminded me of how I might have turned out if Violet Burke hadn't chucked in her job at the munitions factory before I was born.

The female customers fared little better at her

hands; she never tired of warning them that their menfolk could not be trusted and were likely out doing the dirty on them. I was most perturbed on one occasion when Marigold returned from the shop and irrationally started accusing me of all sorts, a bizarre state of affairs since she'd only popped out for some milk.

Despina managed to ignore us whilst simultaneously casting a disparaging look in our direction. Spiros cut to the chase, asking the surly woman if she'd seen his elderly uncle who had gone missing. Her lip actually curled as she curtly responded that she couldn't be expected to know if Spiros' uncle had been in the shop, there were always men coming and going.

Spiros fired back that she could hardly miss his uncle if he'd stopped by since he was out on the streets in nothing but *pitzames kai pantofles*. Recognising the Greek words for pyjamas and slippers I patted myself on the back for paying attention to the chapter on clothing when I'd laboriously pored over my Greek text book. My smug confidence in my Greek language abilities was perhaps a tad misplaced since I failed to comprehend anything beyond the odd expletive in Despina's fiery reply. Stepping back out of range of her sharp tongue I backed into Dimitris, my scholarly friend, lurking inconspicuously next to the barrel of dried cod. Dimitris wasted no time in filling me in on the heated argument by offering a running translation.

"She say to Spiros that she threw from the shop a dirty old bugger indecently dressed in pyjamas who propositioned her," Dimitris hissed. His excellent command of the English language made me reflect that he was certainly benefiting from our doorstep lessons.

"Well he's not exactly got full control of his mental faculties," I said in defence of Leontiades, thinking any man would have had to have taken leave of his senses to proposition the wart faced old harridan.

"Spiros is shouting that she is the liar, he say the uncle would not to proposition her because he is likely the homosexual. He say she have the inflated idea of her own non-existent beauty," Dimitris continued. "He say she is the heartless nasty cow and the person with the compassion would must to recognise the uncle is sickly. Ah, she back down now and change the story, now she say she make the uncle leave because he try to steal."

Spiros' shouted response drowned out Dimitris' translation. As soon as Spiros had finished venting his fury Dimitris filled me in.

"Spiros call her the wicked liar, he say no one in the family ever steal, they have the honest reputation. I have to say Victor this is the true, the Spiros' family is very the honourable, how else would the bereaved trust him with the dead."

"What's she saying now?" I asked, unable to decipher Despina's thick accent.

"She say okay, maybe the uncle not to steal, but he fill the basket with much the shopping then not have the money to pay."

"So first she accuses Leontiades of propositioning her, a fabrication so unlikely I will eat my hat if it's true, then she switches to besmirching the family reputation by calling him a thief," I clarified.

"You have it Victor."

Spiros and Despina were still engaged in a shouting match when Tina arrived, demanding *"Ti symvainei?"* I didn't need Dimitris to translate; I understood Tina had asked 'what's going on?'

Now that Dimitris had translated the gist of the angry exchange I stood back to listen to the whole sorry saga being repeated for Tina's benefit, Despina and Spiros each putting forward their side of the story; it was easier for me to understand on a second hearing. It was pure entertainment gold.

Standing for no nonsense Tina wasted no time in banishing her mother to the storeroom. Apologising profusely to Spiros for her mother's baseless accusations she asked if there was anything she could do to help with finding Leontiades, promising to phone round the village to see if anyone had seen anything of the missing senior after he was slung out of the shop. By the time Barry arrived to say there was no sign of Leontiades in the church, he had missed all the entertainment.

The three of us took the road leading from the village square to the taverna, but no one we passed had seen any sign of Leontiades, most likely otherwise preoccupied with their evening chores. Taking a call on his mobile, Spiros gesticulated for us to carry on searching.

Spiros caught up with us after the call. "That was the Sampaguita."

"Has your uncle returned to the house?" I asked hopefully.

"No, the Sampaguita is just the worried, she care very much for the uncle."

"He's lucky to have a carer who is genuinely fond of him," I said.

"She is the angel. I tell to you Victor the Sampaguita has steal the heart. Since meeting the Sampaguita I have given up the old ways of *kamaki*, the tourist woman no longer turn the head," Spiros confessed.

"*Kamaki?*" Barry repeated, a puzzled expression on his face.

"It's the Greek art of reeling in tourist women for a brief romance," I explained. "I believe it derives from a fishing term."

"Yes, the *kamaki* is to fish for the tourist woman with the chat-up. I think now I to hang up my net," Spiros said, an enamoured expression on his face.

"*Bravo*," I said, pleased that Spiros had finally decided to retire his reputation as a ladies' man, albeit an unsuccessful one, and perhaps settle down.

"You're smitten, Spiro," Barry laughed, thumping the undertaker on the back.

Deciding to separate to expand our search we each took a narrow track or village lane leading from the road. My attention was caught by an old village house, paint peeling from the shutters, the stonework beginning to crumble. I wondered what stories the house could tell and if it would fall into disrepair, or if some foreigner would take pity on it, restoring it to use. Deep purple bougainvillea trailed up one battered wall, bees humming amidst the flowers. Alerted by a rustling noise in the overgrown vegetation to one side of the house I hoped I had discovered Leo's hiding spot. Alas it was nothing but a feral cat pursuing its prey.

Returning to the main street I finally spotted a likely candidate for the missing uncle in Litsa's garden opposite the taverna, a white haired man reclining in a plastic chair stroking a goat, the indomitable Litsa hovering beside him. Presuming there was little doubt that the feeble looking senior clad in slippers and brown checkered pyjamas, the top gaping wide open above a white vest, was indeed the escaped uncle, I hollered out for Barry and Spiros to join me.

Litsa, evidently relieved by our arrival, said she had been at her wits end wondering how to contact Spiros to come and collect his uncle. She told us that she hadn't dared leave him alone whilst she went to a neighbour's house to use the telephone, in case he wandered off again. Litsa revealed Leontiades had been in an agitated state when he turned up, but had apparently found the goat's presence very soothing.

"I go get the hearse to take the uncle home.

Please not to let the uncle out of the sight before I return," Spiros said, planting a kiss on the old chap's head.

Litsa, being inordinately fond of Barry, fussed over him. I tuned out of their stilted conversation, punctuated with many gestures because of the language barrier, my attention riveted on Leontiades. Spiros often spoke of his four uncles, the three deceased ones each having made the undertaker the beneficiary of their homes.

This was the first time I had actually met one of Spiros' relatives, though I did feel I had a good grasp of what Pedros had been like after sifting through the junk he had accumulated in the house which was now ours. Noting the calming effect the goat had on the confused senior I wondered if a feline would have the same soothing impact. I made a mental note to try and persuade Marigold to part with one of the kittens. Surely she could spare one of the little blighters for a good cause; they were no good for anything but getting under my feet and I'd be glad of the opportunity to rid the house of one of the devil spawn of Cynthia's mutant cat Kouneli.

"*Ena toso kalo agori*," Litsa cooed, telling Barry he was such a good boy as she pinched his cheek.

"Keep an eye on the old fellow Victor," Barry

instructed. "I'm just going to pop inside and fix the squeak on Litsa's door; it likely just needs a quick oiling."

"But what if Leo gets agitated again and tries to take off?" I argued.

"A puff of wind would get the better of him, I'm sure you could overpower him if you have to," Barry said, rolling his eyes before disappearing to tackle Litsa's odd-job.

Barry had returned to the garden by the time Spiros rolled up in the hearse. My brother-in-law was loaded up with a carrier bag of Litsa's homemade goodies that the old lady had pressed onto him since he refused to take a cent for fixing her squeak. As the four of us piled into the hearse Barry examined the contents of the carrier bag, proclaiming he would take the tray of *galatopita* along to Doreen's soiree; at least Litsa's milk pudding would provide a palatable dessert to follow Doreen's undoubtedly inedible chicken. It proved a bit of a squash in the hearse but fortunately it was only a short drive back to Spiros' uncle's house, Barry nobly offering his knee to the rather bewildered Leontiades who become a tad teary upon being separated from the goat.

I guessed that the attractive short woman with long dark hair and a contagious smile rushing out of the house to assist Leontiades must be Sampaguita, the fragrant Filipana flower Spiros was so besotted with. "*Imoun toso anisychos gia sena*," she said in extremely clear Greek, gently chiding Leontiades for worrying her. Recalling Marigold telling me that Sampaguita excelled in both Greek and English, I smiled, thinking it was odd that I found her Greek more decipherable than the Greek spoken by many of my Greek neighbours.

"*Elate mesa sto tsai*," Sampaguita said to Leontiades, gesturing for Barry and I to join them, including us in her invitation to drink tea. After settling her elderly charge in a comfortable armchair with a cup of mountain tea, she switched to English, saying "It is my pleasure to meet you Victor and Barry. Spiros tell me you are the good friends. It is so kind of you to help to look for the lost Leo. He gave me the shock when he walk out in the bed clothes. Spiro, I only turn my back for five minutes, I think Leo's mind is deteriorating."

"It is not your fault Sampaguita, I worry the uncle is becoming the more forgetful," Spiros said.

"He was so lucid earlier. How could I even think to go out and leave him this evening? I only left him to put on the dress and he disappeared,"

Sampaguita declared guiltily.

"You shouldn't blame yourself, Marigold's Aunty Beryl had the same condition and could take off at the drop of a hat if no one was watching her closely," I consoled her.

"Of course you must to have the life, before when you go out he has not to be the problem," Spiros said firmly to Sampaguita. "He stay in the chair and not to move when we go to the church on the Sunday."

"I think now it is best not to leave him, he is becoming too vague and must have someone with him all the time," Sampaguita said, her face a picture of worried concern.

"Tomorrow I will put the newspaper advert to find the someone to help you Sampaguita, it is too the much for you to cope alone. I find the someone to look out for the uncle in the night, you must to have the time for yourself," Spiros insisted.

"Please to make sure they have the good recommends, Leo needs a person who will make him feel safe," Sampaguita advised.

"I will," Spiros promised. "Now, we must to hurry to the foreign food, the English watch the clock and think it is the rude to be late."

"Spiro, I cannot leave your uncle alone now,"

Sampaguita protested.

"But I promise to you the exciting night out and you already have the dress on. You cannot to spend all the time caring for the uncle," Spiros said.

"If going out to eat Doreen's chicken is Spiros' idea of an exciting night out then this relationship is doomed," Barry hissed in my ear.

"It may be marginally more exciting than taking her to church which appears to be the extent of their courtship thus far," I hissed back.

"See, the uncle is calm now. He will to sleep if we put him to the bed and give him the night cap," Spiros said, determined to whisk Sampaguita out for the evening.

"Spiro no, I could not enjoy the evening, I would worry all the time about Leo," Sampaguita protested, demonstrating genuine fondness for her charge.

"Then we must to take him with us. The English woman must to have the bed he can sleep on," Spiros decided.

Barry and I exchanged amused glances, imagining Doreen's face when we turned up demanding bed room for a befuddled pyjama clad senior.

Chapter 9

Doreen is Culinary Challenged

T he hearse proved an impossible squash for the five of us and it certainly struck me as inappropriate to offer my knee to Sampaguita on such short acquaintance. Barry and I volunteered to walk across to Doreen's house at the far end of the village, but a call from Marigold to Spiros demanding to know how much longer we were all going to be, led to a change of plan. To save time Barry and I ended up lying down in the back of the plush death cart, huddled together into the space reserved for a coffin, our grimaces reflecting the grim expression of its more usual cargo. When the hearse pulled into the parking space our extremely undignified arrival was clocked by a load of nosy Brits congregated on Doreen's terrace. Fortunately the guests were so distracted by the sight of Barry and me emerging from the back of the hearse like a couple of ghouls that Spiros was able to discreetly slip his uncle indoors, before anyone spotted the old fellow out and about in his bed clothes.

Rushing to greet us with a fake smile, Doreen pulled me aside, hissing, "Really Victor, it's bad enough that you sprang the undertaker and his foreign floozy on me at the last moment, without dragging along half of his relatives."

"Just the one relative actually, Doreen. Sorry but we had no other choice, the old chap's got a touch of dementia and couldn't be left alone in case he tries to escape again," I explained.

"The uncle he just need the nightcap and the bed to sleep," Spiros said sheepishly. Doreen shot a withering look in his direction, having obviously mastered the technique from Marigold.

"Yes, I can see that he's ready for bed. We don't get many callers arriving in their pyjamas," Doreen replied before yelling for Norman to come and show their unwanted guest to a bed.

"I go with them to settle him," Sampaguita offered with a nervous smile.

"Really Victor," Doreen chided. "Your tardiness is most inconvenient; don't blame me if the chicken is dry. No one but you and Barry know that new couple from Nektar, and Norman mistook Frank for a pizza delivery boy when he turned up on the doorstep."

I hazarded a guess. "I take it Frank turned up in Lycra then. I should have mentioned he's a keen cyclist." I wondered if the usually teetotal Norman had been on the booze, imagining pizza delivery boys cycling around a remote Greek village that lacked an actual pizzeria.

"You could have mentioned to Frank that Lycra is hardly the dress code we expect for members of the ex-pat dining club," Doreen replied snootily. She apparently confused the mismatched collection of British thrown together by nothing but village proximity as some kind of representation of colonial throwbacks who must at all cost maintain standards. Clearly I'd let the side down by not mentioning to Frank that Lycra was a tad common.

As I struggled to stop my face from twitching at Doreen's deluded pretentions she sniffed, "Do you even take our little gatherings seriously Victor?" before flouncing off. The woman clearly only tolerates me because of her close friendship with Marigold.

Adopting a put-in-my-place expression I followed Doreen out to the terrace where the rest of the guests were gathered, considering if I looked suitably contrite I might spare myself a tongue lashing from my wife. As it transpired I had misjudged Marigold. Barry had already filled her in on our mission of mercy and it made her a bit weepy, bringing back memories of her now departed Aunty Beryl whom she'd been very fond of.

Everyone was milling around on the terrace sipping drinks. Standing room was in short supply since most of the space was filled with a large trestle table and mismatched chairs. "Aren't those chairs from our kitchen?" I asked Marigold.

"Doreen borrowed a couple, you can hardly expect her to have enough chairs for fourteen people."

Casting my eyes over a set of six chairs that matched the table I made a mental note to avoid them, evidence of the previous night's flight of ants clearly apparent in the unsightly black splotches. Doreen had obviously failed to scrub them clean. I reflected that in addition to being useless in the kitchen our hostess was also a slovenly housekeeper with lax hygiene standards.

"Can't thank you enough for your advice this morning, old chap," Milton boomed, distracting me from the splattered insect corpses as he tapped his nose to indicate it was our little secret that he'd been targeted by scammers. Sidling up next to me he attempted to refill my wine glass.

"No top up for me Milton, thanks," I said, covering my glass with one hand. "I have an early start tomorrow repping on the lazy day cruise."

"Excellent, excellent, I'd try my hand at that myself if it wasn't for the old hip getting a bit wobbly when it's not on dry land."

"Everyone take a seat, dinner is served," Doreen announced.

"Victor, save the chair next to me for the Sampaguita, I go to get her," Spiros pleaded, looking worried they may be separated.

Carefully checking that Norman was nowhere in the near vicinity I claimed three ant free chairs at one end of the table, feeling Sampaguita and Spiros may need my moral support amid the sea of Brits. Winking at me across the table Barry took one for the team, voluntarily electing to sit next to Norman. I reflected that no one could ask for a better brother-in-law. Being blessed with a natural ability to tune out, Barry would be more adept than me at feigning interest when Norman began droning on monotonously about his hobby back in England where he'd been an enthusiastic collector of traffic cones. I certainly knew where I'd be tempted to tell Norman to stick his cones if I had to endure another of his dreary monologues. Moreover Norman demonstrated a complete lack of social grace by never expressing any reciprocal interest in my own prize collection of esoteric back scratchers or my first edition collection of take-away menus.

Approaching the table with Spiros, Sampaguita attracted a lot of interested looks. Although everyone knew the undertaker, few had made the acquaintance of his uncle's carer and appeared curious why she was included in this quintessentially British gathering. Since Meli was a small village where everyone was on top of everyone else's business, it wasn't too surprising that far-fetched rumours abounded.

Even though I'd made a point of squashing any gossip I'd heard about Spiros' wealthy old uncle being shacked up with a young Asian beauty, it didn't put an end to the scurrilous tittle-tattle. Only that week Marigold had got wind that the latest word on the grapevine was that Leontiades had ordered a mail-order bride over the internet and the scheming gold digger was planning to fleece him of every last euro. It seemed clear that some of our fellow diners had heard the rumours but remained oblivious to the truth, appearing curious why the attractive woman who was living with Leontiades was now gadding about the village with his nephew.

"Did you get Leo settled okay?" I asked Sampaguita, inviting her to sit beside me.

"Yes, he is sleeping now. I think his excursion tired him out. I discussed with Spiros and we will take Leo to the hospital soon for the check-up."

Marigold and Edna were giving Doreen a hand in the kitchen. Edna appeared with a basket of bread, followed by Marigold and Doreen carrying trays of starters.

"You're an absolute angel coping with Spiros' sickly uncle, it can't be easy," Marigold praised Sampaguita, passing her an appetizer.

"I hope you're not feeling too hungry," I hissed to Sampaguita, sizing up my miniscule starter. A lump of what appeared to be congealed salad cream covered a decidedly limp looking piece of lettuce in the bottom of a shot glass, three puny prawns balancing on a sliver of lemon hanging over the rim of the glass. It struck me as a travesty that instead of concocting homemade mayonnaise from local extra virgin olive oil and newly laid egg yolks, Doreen resorted to upending an imported bottle of a clearly date-expired condiment. I reflected how much my own tastes had matured since moving to Greece. Recalling how I'd lobbed a bottle of salad cream into the trolley on our last dash round Tesco before emigrating, I winced at the memory of my previously unsophisticated palate.

"What happened to the rest of the prawns, Dor? We haven't got enough here to feed a gnat?" Norman piped up.

"It's not my fault, if everyone had been here on time there would have been an elegant sufficiency of prawns in each cocktail," Doreen said curtly before admitting, "I left the starters out in the kitchen and the cat got into them."

"Literally into the cocktails?" I queried, examining my starter for paw prints.

"Don't be ridiculous Victor, the glasses are much too small for the cat to climb into," Doreen protested.

"I wonder if the cat is still feeling peckish," I hissed to Spiros, hoping I could tempt the feline with the rest of my crustaceans. I certainly had no intention of eating anything Doreen's rather scabby cat may have licked, recalling it wasn't that long since she'd rescued the resident flea infested stray from the village bins.

"It's all very well you putting on airs Victor just because you were paid to snoop round in restaurant kitchens, but I heard you weren't so fussy when you were serving up snails," Doreen snapped.

"The gastropods I gathered for my *saliggaria stifado* are considered a local delicacy, at least they didn't come out of Lidl's frozen food section like these prawns," I retorted, bristling at Doreen's lack of appreciation for the importance of my career as a public health inspector.

"Anyone for more wine?" Barry interrupted, attempting to diffuse the tense moment. With Doreen temporarily distracted I took the opportunity to sling my prawns to the cat, their cold clammy texture making me think *good grief the wretched woman hasn't even mastered the art of defrosting properly*. My heart sank as I watched Marigold tuck into her prawn cocktail with gusto; I hoped she wasn't going to suffer with a dicky tummy later.

Doreen was obviously keen to hurry everyone along with their prawn cocktails, needing to rescue the chicken parmesan before it dried up beyond redemption in the oven. Whisking away the shot glasses she fired an accusatory look in my direction. Doreen apparently held me responsible for the detritus of rejected prawns lurking in the bottom of most of the other guests' glasses, beneath scrumpled paper napkins. I considered it a bit rich that she couldn't take responsibility for her own culinary shortcomings, obviously defeated by the challenge of coping with a bottle of salad cream and a bag of frozen prawns.

Edna and Marigold both went to Doreen's assistance, dishing the chicken parmesan up and helping to distribute plates of food around the table. Spiros put a restraining hand on Sampaguita's arm when she stood up to help, telling her to relax and enjoy the evening. With everyone served and the wine flowing freely, Barry announced to the table that he'd bought Harold's house, creating a flurry of interest.

"You and Vangelis are certainly skilled enough to transform the place," Julie said. She and Frank had rejected the house out of hand, considering the level of work necessary to restore the traditional features was too much for part-time residents to take on.

"Odd chap that Harold, very boorish, never

fitted into the village. I'll be glad to see the back of him," Milton said. "I do hope he takes that monstrous satellite dish with him when he goes, it's a total eyesore."

"He's leaving it behind, but I've no use for it," Barry said. "Spiros is going to take it off my hands."

Everyone fired disgruntled looks at Spiros, preferring that the unsightly satellite dish be banished to the tip. There was visible relief when Barry clarified, "No one will see the dish, there's a discreet spot for it at the back of Spiros' uncle's house."

"With the technology satellite the Sampaguita will to be able to watch the favourite television she miss from the home," Spiros explained, Sampaguita smiling shyly beside him. His words opened the door for our fellow diners to unleash their curiosity about his companion.

"Where is it that you're from, dear?" Doreen asked. The way she over enunciated her vowels came across as a tad patronising; she clearly expected Sampaguita to struggle with English.

"The Philippines," Sampaguita replied, blushing slightly at being the centre of attention. "It will help me to feel a little less homesick to watch Eat Bulaga! It is a very popular programme at home, next year it will be twenty five years it has been on the television."

"Ah, a bit like our Corrie, that's been on the go forever too," Doreen replied.

"Do you miss home very much? You must do, with being on your own in a strange country. I have my Milton and of course all my English friends in the village, but you must be a bit like a duck out of water with being foreign," Edna said to Sampaguita, completely overlooking the obvious fact that she herself was a foreigner in Greece.

"Spiros and his uncle are very kind and make me feel at home..."

"And the age difference doesn't bother you?" Doreen asked.

"I don't understand," Sampaguita stammered.

"Living with a much older man," Doreen clarified, determined to get the lowdown. Spiros' snort brought her up short.

"The Sampaguita is employ to care for the old and infirm uncle, she has much the skill with the sickly, and the excellent recommends. I think Doreen you have been to listen to the stupid rumour that the uncle take the young girlfriend," Spiros said. Pausing for effect, his eyes scanned the table. "Perhaps you not to hear the rumour that the uncle is likely the homosexual."

"Sampaguita is an absolute treasure, the way she cares for Leo goes way beyond professionalism," Marigold said as Doreen turned puce. "It's always such a worry hoping that the carers looking after our elderly genuinely care."

"I am fond of Leo, it makes it easier to be separated from my children to know I can help. I do miss my family very much but the money I earn means my children can have the good education," Sampaguita explained.

"You should get your husband to pull his weight," Norman tactlessly interjected.

"It would be the difficult as he is been the dead for the decade," Spiros snapped.

"That's a bit of a rough deal, having to work abroad and being separated from your kiddies," Frank observed sympathetically.

"Many people in my country work overseas to give our families the better life. My children are almost grown now, Jasmine is training to be a nurse and Joy has the dream to become the doctor. Jayson likes nothing more than to help his grandfather on the farm, he is the strong boy," Sampaguita said, her deep brown eyes shining with pride.

"But you look so young to have three almost

grown children, I'd have guessed you were in your early twenties if it wasn't verbatim to speak of a woman's age," Milton said.

"You are very kind," Sampaguita replied.

"You must call in for a cup of tea, dear," Edna invited. "I expect you must find it difficult making friends, what with being foreign."

"People are very kind. It is hard to go out because Leo takes much caring for, but Marigold came to the house to welcome me to the village, and Dina and Athena both call in often for a visit. Papas Andreas is very kind when he visits Leo. I like very much when Kyria Kompogiannopoulou comes to the house because she brings her little grandson to play, he is so cute and I just love children," Sampaguita said.

"But it must be difficult for you trying to communicate with the Greeks when they visit you," Doreen said.

"Not at all, we speak together in Greek," Sampaguita said, shaming Doreen into silence.

"Ah bravo, you've mastered the old lingo," Milton boomed. "I'd make more of an effort myself if it wasn't so blasted difficult for us oldies to pick it up."

"We're dreading the thought of having to get to grips with Greek, but we know we ought to make the effort," Julie said, Frank nodding along in agreement

"I wonder if we should get a satellite dish, Norman," Doreen suggested, pointedly changing the subject. "We could catch up with Corrie on those long winter evenings."

"It looks like we don't really need the old telly for a bit of entertainment," Milton boomed. I squirmed in my seat, hoping this wasn't the moment that Milton decided to make a public declaration about his secret life writing porn. Fortunately I had jumped to a hasty assumption. The entertainment Milton referred to was the sudden appearance of Spiros' uncle Leontiades looking completely befuddled as he wandered out onto the terrace, Doreen's scabby cat perched comfortably on his head as though it was the latest must-have fashion accessory.

Shaking his head in confusion Leo said "*Pou einai to kapelo mou?*" asking where his hat was. Spiros jumped to his feet, assuring his uncle that his hat was safely on his head, gently trying to steer him away from the gawping glances and back into the spare bedroom. Just as I was wondering if this was the right moment to suggest to Marigold that we donate one of the kittens to Leo as an emotional support animal, Doreen's cat regurgitated the dodgy prawns down the front of Leo's pyjamas.

Chapter 10

Dinner Table Obsessions

Doreen, I didn't realise you had your father staying, why on earth isn't the old chap joining us for dinner?" Milton said as Spiros led his uncle away.

"He's nothing to do with me, he turned up with the undertaker," Doreen protested.

"Ah quite, nice chap the undertaker, nothing is too much trouble for him. He insisted on collecting my prescription from the pharmacy to save me wear and tear on the old hip, most obliging of him," Milton said.

"This is delicious chicken, you must give me the recipe," Julie gushed. Looking down at my chicken parmesan I considered Julie's compliment odd in the extreme. She was either attempting to curry favour with our hostess or an unfortunate accident had deprived her of the use of her taste buds. In truth the poultry dish was exactly the sort of thrown together mess I had anticipated, a lump of anaemic looking chicken coated in soggy breadcrumbs, swimming around in a red sauce that bore an uncanny resemblance to tinned tomato soup. A clump of stringy cheese bearing not the slightest resemblance to the parmesan the dish was named for, topped the foul concoction.

The stench of garlic was overpowering, but Doreen explained it away by admitting her hand had slipped when she tipped in the garlic powder. I recoiled in shock at her admission; it wasn't exactly as though we were living in an era of rationing where one had to add nasty substitute powders to the pan. Surely the woman could have cultivated some fresh garlic in her garden if she felt deterred from buying fresh garlic bulbs in the shop by Despina sounding off about Norman's imagined infidelity.

After examining the chicken with the tine of

my fork, I looked around in vain for the cat before recalling Leo had confused it with a hat. I had no intention of subjecting myself to a likely dose of food poisoning by risking the rather green hued chicken, though I had to admit it was quite a remarkable feat to produce chicken that was simultaneously raw yet as dry as old shoe leather.

Sampaguita, appearing equally unimpressed with the poor excuse for a chicken dinner, whispered to me that Spiros had promised he was taking her out for *pitsa*.

"Oh, how could I be so forgetful, I left the spaghetti that goes with the chicken in the microwave," Doreen said. As she rushed into the kitchen it left the coast clear to tip the revolting contents of my plate into the plastic bag I had secreted in my pocket earlier, anticipating just such an eventuality. Sampaguita stared at me enviously before hurriedly passing me her plate, her relief evident that I had provided a suitable disposable receptacle for the strange foreign food.

"Quick Victor, pass that over here," Barry said, scraping the contents of his and Cynthia's plates into the bag.

"Is that a doggy bag?" Milton asked. "Excellent, if nobody minds we'll take that home with us for tomorrow's lunch, it will save the odd bob or two on the old food bill."

I pondered the wisdom of offering my sound advice on the perils of eating Doreen's dodgy chicken, but decided to keep my own counsel. It wouldn't do to get a reputation as an interfering know-it-all. Besides I reasoned that Milton and Edna had survived living in some remote part of Africa where hygiene inspections weren't really a thing.

Doreen cast a suspicious glance at my empty plate when she returned bearing the spaghetti, but wisely chose to bite her tongue. Conversation resumed around the dinner table, with Harold's swimming pool now the topic of interest.

"I'm surprised you want to take on a pool of that size, old chap. It will be a dreadful bother, all those chemicals you have to mess about with," Milton boomed. I noticed his voice was getting considerably louder over the course of the evening but considered it wasn't my place to suggest he turn his hearing aid up.

"It's an expensive business maintaining a pool," Frank piped up.

"Not to mention the ghastly bother of fishing dead pigeons and sheep out of it," Milton said, his comment eliciting a collection of bemused expressions.

"And there's the worry of keeping it hidden from the tax inspectors, Norman said.

"We have no intention of keeping the swimming pool, we plan to transform it into an ecological pond, it will be so environmentally friendly," Cynthia said smugly.

"So you'll just leave any dead sheep that fall in to decompose naturally?" Milton asked.

"I honestly hadn't given any thought to the possible drowning of any passing livestock, the pool area is walled," Cynthia said.

"But a wall won't keep pigeons out, they could dive splat into your pond," Milton insisted, seemingly obsessed with random pigeons dropping out of the sky.

"We had a sheep get into our courtyard last week, we couldn't persuade it to leave, it just stood there refusing to budge," Edna said, perhaps explaining the couple's sudden obsession with intrusive livestock. "It penned me in the kitchen and wouldn't let me get to the washing line. You should have seen the size of its horns."

"You should be glad it was a sheep and not a goat. A goat would have chomped its way through any washing on your line," Barry laughed, perhaps recalling Vangelis' borrowed goat making a meal out of his jeans.

"It wasn't funny, I was at my wit's end. I tried to shoo it away but it just held its ground, looking at me with a demonic stare. I was terrified it would try to head-butt me with its fearsome horns," Edna insisted.

"That fellow who wanders round in wellies in all weathers had to come and fetch it," Milton said, presumably referring to Panos. "Had a hell of a bother communicating with the old chap, he doesn't speak a word of English."

"Milton had to baa at him, to make him understand about the sheep. Baa, baa," Edna said, emulating the bleating call of a sheep just in case any of us were clueless what they sounded like.

"Actually sheep can swim so you needn't worry about one drowning in your pond," Julie said to Cynthia. "I must say an ecological pond sounds lovely, very at one with nature."

"It will be a haven for birds and bats attracted to a natural water source filled with aquatic plants," Cynthia said.

"I hope it doesn't attract any frogs, the last thing we want to put up with is a daily chorus of croaking," Doreen complained.

"I'm not sure swapping the pool for a pond is wise, you have to consider it may be detrimental to the house price," Norman said. "You have to consider the re-sale value."

"I'll just go and see if Spiros needs a hand with his uncle," I said abruptly, amazed we had almost managed to make it to the dessert course without the inevitable topic of house prices cropping up. I knew from experience that the rest of the evening would be hogged by Norman offering a painful dissection of the most miniscule shift in property prices back in England. To be fair to my fellow countrymen most of them would just grin and bear the tedious topic as Norman got carried away with his obsession. I'd learned to my peril that the only sure fire way of getting him off the subject was to start banging on about traffic cones.

Spiros was standing just outside the front door, enveloped in a plume of smoke from his cigarette.

"I feel the bad for the Sampaguita, this is not the *romantikos* evening I hope for," he said.

As I'd been the one to extend the invitation for Spiros to join us, I felt a tad guilty, even though I was certain I hadn't hinted an evening at the ex-pat dining club would be romantic.

"I have a free evening tomorrow when I've finished with the lazy day cruise. How about I babysit your uncle so you can take Sampaguita out somewhere nice, just the two of you?" I suggested, thinking perhaps he could woo her over a candlelit dinner away from the village.

"You would do that for me, Victor."

"I'm only sorry I didn't think of it sooner," I said, happy to give the course of true love a fighting chance. I didn't anticipate the uncle would give me any trouble if I kept the doors locked, and I could use the evening to pen another chapter of the book in peace.

"You are the good friend," Spiros said. "I hope I can find easily the person to help with the uncle, it is not many that want to work in the village such the distance from the town."

"Perhaps one of the Greek ladies in the village would be willing to help out," I suggested. "Before you hired Sampaguita you said that the local ladies would be wary of ruining their reputations by moving into the house with your uncle, but now you have Sampaguita living in..."

"And the Sampaguita will protect the reputation of the Greek woman helper. Victor, you are the genius," Spiros declared, depositing a smacker of a kiss on my forehead.

"I'm only sorry that Sampaguita has had to suffer her own reputation being besmirched by gossip," I said.

"The Sampaguita may look the fragile but she have the back of steel, she have no concern for the petty gossip."

"Ah, a steely backbone always comes in useful," I agreed. I recalled the steely resolve I'd been forced to draw on when the jumped-up Greek-Cypriot owner of a chippy with delusions of Michelin star abilities, and grand ambitions to expand into an up-market fish and chip restaurant, threatened to douse me with a bucket of batter. I refused to back down and turn a blind eye to his gross hygiene violations. By my next inspection his rating jumped from a two to a four, not because he had intimidated me, but because knowing I meant business he had spent every spare minute scrubbing the place. My ruminations were interrupted by the sound of approaching footsteps.

"What are you two doing skulking out here? Spiros, you shouldn't have left that charming young lady alone with us all, she may find us a bit intimidating," Doreen said, her tone much friendlier now that she'd downed half a bottle of wine. "I must say your uncle seems very attached to the cat, he wasn't fazed at all when it threw up all over him. I do hope he doesn't find it too upsetting when he has to leave it behind when you take him home."

Slipping my arm around Doreen's shoulder I whispered conspiratorially, "Perhaps you could help me to butter Marigold up enough so that she'd be willing to part with one of our kittens. I think an emotional support animal is just what Leo needs and you know how much my wife values your opinion."

Doreen stared at me suspiciously for a moment, more accustomed to being on the receiving end of my sarcasm rather than flattering words.

"You do have a surfeit of the creatures. I'm always saying to Marigold that one cat per household is quite sufficient to keep the place mouse free. Any more than a couple and one runs the risk of being labelled a mad cat woman," Doreen said. Patting my arm she assured me, "You can leave it with me Victor. Now do come back to the table, I'm about to dish up the pudding. Norman's sister sent us some Angle Delight over from England."

"Not more of the horrible food," Spiros hissed to me as we followed Doreen back to the group.

"Don't worry, we can fill up on the *galatopita* Litsa gave Barry," I said, looking forward to the delicious Greek pudding.

Chapter 11

A Fearsome Obstruction

The light of the full moon cast a silvery reflection over the sea as we strolled home, cicadas serenading us in the breezeless night.

"I came this close to suggesting where Norman could stick his traffic cones," Marigold giggled, holding her finger and thumb apart. "Thank goodness you're doing the lazy day cruise in the morning so we had an excuse to leave early."

"I thought you enjoyed the ex-pat dining club evenings, you're the one who always insists we show up."

"We have to make an effort to be sociable Victor. It wouldn't do to be social outcasts like Harold and Joan, but in truth I find it much more relaxing to spend an evening in the taverna. Shall we go there tomorrow? You won't feel much like cooking after being on the boat all day and Athena's doing my roots in her kitchen, so I won't be in the mood to cook."

"We'll have to make it another night darling, I promised Spiros I'd sit with his uncle so he can take Sampaguita out for a romantic evening," I said.

"She could certainly use one; I didn't know where to look when Doreen started implying the poor girl was carrying on with Spiros' old uncle. Perhaps I'll come along with you, it depends if Cynthia has plans, it's all getting a bit on top of me having the four of us living together."

This was obviously a dig at Cynthia since Marigold was in her element having Barry under our roof.

"It's not for long now," I assured her, thinking it wouldn't be long at all until the four of us morphed into seven under one roof. I'd be quite tempted to volunteer to take the overnight shift babysitting Leo when our houseguests arrived, but no doubt Marigold would start muttering about the divorce courts if I took off and left her to cope with Violet Burke.

"Oh Victor, do smell this lavender," Marigold said, breaking a stem from the intoxicating plant surrounding Kyria Kompogiannopoulou's doorway. "We must pop up to Lefteris' garden centre in town and buy some for the garden. I read that lavender is a natural mosquito deterrent because they detest the scent."

"They're supposed to loath Marmite but it never stops them from draining my blood no matter how much I rub into my exposed bits," I replied.

"Well at least with the Marmite you don't stink like a chip shop, like Barry with his vinegar. If we bought some lavender plants from Lefteris I could soak the flowers in oil and experiment with making you some homemade mosquito repellent."

"Or perhaps Kyria Kompogiannopoulou could give us a lavender cutting rather than us traipsing up to the garden centre," I deliberately teased Marigold. I was quietly envious of my wife who rarely suffered a bite. In contrast the hovering blighters delighted in feasting on my blood. Conventional remedies didn't help, anything containing even a drop of DEET bringing me out in an allergic reaction resembling hives.

I found it quite amusing that Marigold was scrambling for an excuse to call into the garden centre. My wife had developed a mild crush on the tattooed and leather clad young man with the pampered pet poodle Fufu, ever since he had whisked her off for coffee when they ran into each other in the veterinarian's waiting room. Of course it was all perfectly innocent and didn't threaten my manhood; it was only natural for a woman of Marigold's age to feel flattered when a handsome younger man showered her with polite, if insincere, attention.

Suddenly Marigold screamed in alarm, clutching my arm in a vice- like grip and pointing a quivering finger towards the dark cobbled alleyway that ran down one side of Kyria Kompogiannopoulou's house. "Victor, there's something lurking in the shadows," she cried, her voice suddenly hoarse with fear.

"It's probably nothing, maybe Guzim is taking a shortcut to his shed," I reassured Marigold, though an icy shiver ran down my spine. I released a nervous laugh when the lurking figure moved directly into our path, the moonlight revealing a bulky horned figure. I exhaled in relief when I saw it was simply a sheep, but my hackles rose when the sheep proved to be obstructive, obstinately refusing to budge or let us pass.

"Do something Victor, its eyes look demonic," Marigold hissed.

"Nonsense, it's likely a docile domestic that has wandered off."

"It looks like it could do someone an injury with those horns and I don't like the way its baring its teeth, what if it moves in for the bite?"

"Marigold, get a grip, sheep don't wander about biting humans, they are herbivores," I said, wondering if it would alarm my wife unduly if I mentioned they were prone to a spot of head-butting, particularly during the rutting season. Since I was clueless if the obstructive creature was in the mating mood I thought it best not to mention its possible propensity for using its skull as a weapon, and I certainly had no desire to experience an up close and personal encounter with its horns.

"With all the scrawny sheep about it's a bit much that we get obstructed by one that appears to have been fattened up," Marigold said.

"Don't worry darling, just keep hold of my arm and we'll edge into the road and step by it," I advised, thinking it was quite ludicrous that we felt threatened by a sheep.

As we stepped from the narrow pavement into the road, the sheep mirrored our move, standing stubbornly in front of us with no intention of moving. I regretted letting Milton make off with the bag of rejected food since it could have served as a handy weapon to swing at the sheep.

"It's probably got separated from its flock. The decent thing to do would be to ring Panos and see if he's missing one," I said, beginning to sense the animal would indeed resort to a spot of head-butting if we made any sudden movements.

I could hear the sound of Nikos playing the bouzouki in the background when I connected with Panos. He was obviously enjoying an evening at the taverna. I belatedly realised I faced the challenge of conversing in telephone Greek, something I still dreaded, finding it difficult to communicate in a foreign language when I was unable to study the other person's face.

Panos appeared delighted, although somewhat surprised, to hear from me. He immediately launched into extended and convoluted Greek pleasantries, first enquiring about my health, before asking after Marigold, then Barry, and then about my homosexual son back in England. Before he could ask about the well-being of the cats

I interrupted, telling him there was a sheep blocking the road and asking if he was missing one.

Speaking very slowly as if to an imbecile, Panos asked me what the sheep looked like, "*Pos moiazei?*"

"*Moiazei me provato,*" I replied, telling him it looked like a sheep. Realising that wasn't particularly helpful, I added, "*einai agori,*" meaning it's a boy, unable to recall the Greek word for a ram. I had definitely learnt it at some point, but retaining so many new foreign words was proving more of a challenge than I'd anticipated.

"What's he saying," Marigold badgered.

"He says we should stay with it and he'll be right along."

"It's not as though we have any choice in the matter, the stubborn creature isn't going to let us by," Marigold said, pointing out the obvious. "I do hope Panos hurries up, I'm in rather desperate need of the loo."

The creak of a wooden shutter being thrust open attracted our attention and we looked up to see Kyria Kompogiannopoulou poking her head out of an upstairs window. "*Ti symvainei?*" she shouted, demanding to know what was going on.

"*Kalispera Kyria,*" I called up, having no intention of attempting to pronounce her complete tongue-twister of a name. *"Ena provato einai sto dromo,"* I said, telling her there was a sheep in the road.

Instead of replying she simply clicked her tongue in the Greek habit of expressing disdain.

"Do ask her if I can use her toilet, Victor," Marigold pleaded, prompting a replica tut from my own lips.

The front door was thrown open by Kyria Kompogiannopoulou, arms tightly folded across the bosom of her dressing gown, a deep scowl etched on her features. Peering at us through narrowed eyes she assessed the situation, saying *"fovasai ena provato,"* before dissolving into helpless laughter at the very notion we were afraid of the sheep. Marigold bowled past her, muttering *"I toualeta parakalo."* Fortunately the elderly lady was on familiar terms with Marigold since they both attended the monthly meetings to beautify the cemetery. Shrugging my shoulders I tried to convey the impression it was perfectly normal for my wife to be caught short after being confronted by an aggressive sheep.

By the time Marigold sheepishly reappeared from the toilet Panos had turned up to lead the recalcitrant animal away. Marigold and I were the butt of his humour as he exploded with laughter, making no effort to contain his mirth as he told Kyria Kompogiannopoulou *"fovountai ena provato,"* completely incredulous that we were apparently afraid of the sheep.

"Well at least we've given the villagers something new to gossip about tomorrow, instead of Sampaguita," I said to Marigold, certain Panos wouldn't be able to resist making fun at our expense.

"If he dares to breathe one word we should report him to the authorities for failing to keep control of a dangerous animal," Marigold replied huffily.

"Oh come on Marigold, you have to see the funny side, it was only a sheep, we probably overreacted," I said, releasing my nervous tension in laughter.

My laughter proved contagious: Marigold joined in, finally saying between bouts of guffawing, "How about you knock up a mutton curry next week?"

Chapter 12

The End of an Orange Era

Even though I crept from my bed at the crack of dawn, the path to the bathroom still resembled Piccadilly Circus, Cynthia and Barry both having early starts along with myself. Only Marigold, with nothing on her agenda more taxing than having her roots touched up, could afford an indulgent lie-in. My annoyance at emerging from the shower to discover Cynthia had failed to rinse through the drip-dry bright orange polyester rep tee-shirt she had borrowed was tempered by Barry having already brewed a pot of hot aromatic coffee. I needed to don the hideous orange shirt for the lazy day cruise: all the tour company employees were expected to ritually humiliate themselves by turning out looking as though they'd just been tangoed. I was in no mood to receive a dressing down from Tiffany, the English supervisor who was less than half my age, if she were to discover I had violated the strict uniform policy.

Cynthia dragged herself into the kitchen blearily rubbing sleep from her eyes, her glossy hair all askew, making a beeline for the coffee. She was definitely not a morning person.

"It's really not good enough Cynthia, I lent you my shirt after you scorched yours irreparably with the iron, the least you could do was rinse it out," I snapped.

"What's that Victor, just let me get some caffeine down," Cynthia replied, seemingly oblivious to my shirtless plight as she gulped a large mug of coffee. With the caffeine fix inside her she said, "Oh yes, I forgot to tell you yesterday, we've been issued new uniforms. The persistent complaints you stuffed into the staff suggestion box about being forced to wear unflattering and unbreathable orange polyester paid off. I knew you didn't need to go into the office before your boat trip today so I brought your new uniform home with me, you just need to sign that you've received it next time you go into the office."

Cynthia disappeared into the spare bedroom, returning with three sealed cellophane packages she handed to me. As I tore the packages open Cynthia commented, "See no more polyester, these are made from modacrylic, whatever that is."

"It is flame resistant acrylic," I told her, thinking the fabric was at least a slight improvement, even if it wasn't ideal for hot weather. The white polo shirt I unwrapped was emblazoned with a large Greek flag: a pair of navy knee-length shorts, and a matching white cap boasting a smaller flag, completed the uniform. "I'll go and change."

Posing in front of the mirror I decided the new uniform gave me a decidedly debonair air; in addition it made me feel patriotic, even though the label clearly stated Made in China. I was gratified that my suggestion box ideas had been influential rather than ignored. Rejoicing at the end of the orange era, I sighed with relief that I would no longer need to suffer being an orange indignity.

"Very smart," Barry said in approval when I

returned to the kitchen. Cynthia, now beginning to feel human, let loose with a wolf whistle.

"That could be construed as work place harassment," I joked.

"I don't think it counts when I harass you at home," Cynthia teased. "Oh by the way, I forgot to mention, Tiffany was desperate for someone to lead a new tour that starts this week. I thought it would be right up your alley so I signed you up. I'd have claimed first dibs myself but I don't dare risk piling on extra kilos before the wedding in case I can't get into my dress."

"A new tour?" I queried sharply, thinking Cynthia had taken an unspeakable liberty by not discussing it with me first. Her high-handed approach reminded me of the blasé way Marigold had volunteered me as skivvying chef without first consulting me.

"You'll love it Victor, it involves guiding a small group around the market and specialist food shops in town, introducing them to the gastronomic delights of Greece. Since it clashes with your guided tour of Ancient Olympia Tiffany will have to find some other mug to traipse round the Olympic hell.

"Cynthia, I could kiss you," I said. "Thank goodness you realised I am of course the natural choice to lead a foodie experience, it sounds very cultured. I'm so happy you didn't hesitate to sign me up."

The fact that the new tour clashed with the Olympia excursion meant I would be released from the weekly hellish trip. My initial enthusiasm for guiding tourists around Ancient Olympia had very soon waned, each excursion attracting at least one little Johnny who drove me to the limits of my breaking point. I sometimes speculated if the seemingly endless supply of random little Johnnies and sex-starved women determined to make Sakis their holiday conquest, were company plants, rather like mystery shoppers.

"I can see that living here has given you an appreciation of my culinary knowledge, making it obvious a man of my refinement would be an excellent fit as a foodie guide," I said to Cynthia.

"Oh no, it wasn't that," Cynthia replied. "I thought with your food hygiene background you'd be able to warn the tourists if any of the food looked a bit dodgy. Tiffany was a bit worried we might get sued if anyone came down with food poisoning."

The drive up to town was absolutely glorious. The early start was necessary since I needed to be at the gangplank at oh-nine-hundred hours sharp to greet the tourists. I always find it preferable to drive up to town just after sunrise as the July heat can sap all the energy from one's body later. Although I would be unable to avoid the heat on the drive home later I considered I may indulge in the luxury of air conditioning at Spiros' uncle's house that evening. Though naturally wary of the hazards posed by clogged up units recirculating tainted air, I had noticed that Sampaguita kept an impeccably clean house. Leo's mental deterioration wasn't the sort of contagious condition one could catch through a cooling vent.

I realised that I would need to spend the evening swatting up on specialist Greek culinary delights, rather than penning the latest chapter of the book. Obviously anyone signing up for the gastronomic tour would expect me to be an authority on the subject, able to school them in the difference between *mizithra* and *manouri* cheeses, and impart fun and fascinating facts about Greek aphrodisiacs. Unfortunately an-over reliance on Nikos' *spitiko* and the plastic bottled offerings from the village store left my knowledge of Greek wines with a gaping hole. I decided to pick Dimitris' brain before my first tour. Although my professor friend didn't strike me as an oenophile he would likely be well versed in anything the ancient Greeks had written on the subject of wine. Of course there was also a passing chance that Vasos, the ex-navy Greek who captained the lazy day cruise boat, may have a passable knowledge of Greek wine. He certainly enjoyed a drink.

It struck me as ironic that the word passable had just flitted through my mind, since the road up to town was anything but. I'd had the misfortune to get stuck behind the early morning bus, traffic coming towards me making it impossible to overtake. The impassable road reminded me of the sheep block the previous evening and I speculated if I was now the laughing stock of the village or if Panos would have spared my pride by not spreading the word that I'd been unnerved by a sheep.

Finally the bus pulled over to pick up some passengers, allowing me to put my foot down and overtake. With the windows down to the hilt I revelled in the warm breeze in my hair, spontaneously bursting into song as the familiar refrain of the 2001 Eurovision chart topper 'Die for You' played over the radio. I reflected how much my life had changed since moving to Greece. Before I took early retirement I would have spent the best part of my morning stuck in endless traffic jams, driving between a seemingly endless chain of clean or thoroughly grotty kitchens; yet here I was now with a new lease of life, about to start my working day aboard a lazy day pleasure cruise on the Mediterranean.

Chapter 13

Crewing the Pleasure Boat

Vasos was nowhere to be seen when I arrived at the boat, Pegasus, moored in the harbour. Fortunately the gangplank was down, so I made my way on board clutching my satchel containing the paperwork pertaining to that day's trip. With forty-five tourists signed up for the cruise it shouldn't be too much of a scrum if some of them elected to sunbathe on the upper deck, rather than sitting around on the wooden benches lining the main deck.

V.D. BUCKET

Pleased to note that everything appeared to be in shipshape order, I stuck my head in the toilet to give it the once over. The on-deck lavatory was the one area of the boat that routinely received negative feedback on the customer satisfaction survey. Noting with disgust that the floor was awash with water, that the toilet-paper bin was overflowing, and that no effort had been made to fix the temperamentally dodgy toilet chain, I decided to hunt down Sami, Captain Vasos' sidekick and sea-faring helper.

I didn't need to hunt far; Sami was shuffling along the deck, his head slumped in his typical hangdog style. He dragged a mop and bucket along in his wake, a cigarette clamped between his lips, another one conveniently tucked behind his ears ready to be lit from the current dog end. I would love to regale my readers with a true account of Sami's fascinating past. However whatever information I have gleaned about him came second-hand from Vasos, so may be a tad unreliable and should be taken with a pinch of salt.

Captain Vasos speaks not a word of English, but his Greek is generally decipherable since he sticks to a simple vocabulary and bellows every word at a level that threatens the decibel scale, a habit he developed during his long navy stint in order to be heard over the din of the ship's engines. I particularly appreciate Vasos' ability to immediately spot when I am flummoxed by the meaning of a Greek word. I can see the cogs turning in his alcohol fuddled brain as he searches for another way to express what he is saying; Vasos may be half-cut half the time, but he is keen to be understood. Anyway, back to Sami's intriguing life story as relayed to me second-hand by a rather unreliable alcoholic.

Apparently no one ever knew Sami's real name, and being mute he was unable to reveal it himself. In addition to his real identity, his age remains a mystery because no one can recall exactly what year it was, decades ago, when he was fished out of the Aegean by a passing naval vessel. The sailors on-board the ship apparently took an instant liking to the rescued lad due to his remarkable feat of bravery in keeping a firm grasp on the bedraggled, half-drowned soggy cat he was holding aloft in the water, the cat reputedly so cute it melted the hardest of hearts. Rumours persist that the rescue may have been enacted during wartime, but this could just be poetic embellishment to put a more interesting twist on the story.

The castaway was assumed to be a fellow

Greek as he clearly understood the language. Since he couldn't speak or pen more than a cross, he was christened with the name Sami in honour of the nearest landmark, the Island of Samothrace. Rumour has it that when the ship turned course with the intention he would be dropped off at the nearest spot of dry land, Sami chained himself to the mast, shaking his head like a madman and screaming silently.

Loathe to subject the youngster to whatever hellish existence he had escaped from, the sailors kept him on-board, adopting the mute boy as their ship mascot and making his feline friend the honorary ship's cat. In gratitude for not being jettisoned from the ship, Sami took to swabbing the decks and general skivvying with an enthusiasm that drew the respect of the hardened crew. Sami's feet didn't touch dry land for years, according to Vasos. These days he ventures ashore in the captain's company, though it has to be said he no longer mops with enthusiasm. Decades of exposure to the sea and elements have left Sami's lined features rough and weatherworn. He may well be younger than his appearance suggests but if I was to hazard a guess it may be wide of the mark; he could be anything from fifty to seventy-five.

Ever since Vasos had acquired Pegasus, Sami had crewed for him. Vasos had amassed a considerable pot of cash during his stint in the merchant navy, saving every cent he didn't squander on ouzo and a girl in every port. After leaving the navy at the age of fifty Vasos still needed to earn his crust. Splurging his cash on Pegasus fulfilled his life-long dream of a life on the ocean waves, with no officious commanding officer rationing his ouzo intake. The idea of offering tourist trips on his boat struck him as ideal; six months of staying just sober enough to steer the boat, followed by six months of lazing around, licentious carousing, and promiscuity, or at least in his dreams.

Drawing level with Sami on the deck I told him the toilet was filthy. "*Tin toualeta einai vromiko.*" Unable to answer he gestured over one shoulder with his thumb, indicating he was onto it with the mop and bucket. "*Kathe ora katharizete,*" I added, advising him mop it out every hour; there was nothing worse than expecting paying tourists to paddle their way through a mess of floating toilet paper whenever they got caught short. Sami responded by holding one finger in front of my face, a gesture I found it hard to interpret, wondering if he was trying to tell me he would only clean the toilet once or agreeing to mop it every hour. Fortunately I noticed he wasn't attempting to communicate using only his little finger, an insulting gesticulation that Spiros had warned me was used as a way of saying one had a small joystick. Responding with a thumbs-up, I went off in search of Vasos.

I found the captain in the wheel house. Though on first glance it appeared to be empty, the thunderous snoring and the pungent stink of sweat coming from under a rancid pile of un-washed towels gave away Vasos' location. With the tourists due to arrive within the half-hour Vasos' deep slumber wasn't a good sign. "Vaso, *xypna*," I shouted, kicking the pile of laundry with my foot to encourage him to wake up. I had no intention of soiling my hands by shaking him awake, his tee-shirt so stiff with sweat it could probably stand up on its own. "*Xypna, ora ya dou-lei*," 'wake up, it's time to work.'

The pile of laundry slowly unfurled, reveal-ing Vasos' unshaven face. "Victor," Vasos rasped in a voice hoarse from too many cigarettes and too much ouzo, seemingly shocked by my pres-ence. Grubbing around for a dog end in the over-flowing ashtray, he asked me the time, "*ti ora einai*?"

"Ora ya doulei," I replied, telling him it was time for work.

Forcing himself to a sitting position Vasos raised his arms above his head. Stretching and yawning he stripped off his tee-shirt before standing up and removing his shorts without a trace of embarrassment. Wrapping a soiled towel around his midriff he finally covered his modesty before shuffling off towards the toilet, clutching a bar of soap and muttering the single word *"dous."* Considering the on-board toilet didn't actually contain a shower I surmised he planned to splash water from the sink over his body; that would at least account for the permanently underwater state of the toilet floor. I made a mental note to tell Sami to give it another mopping before the first tourists stepped on board.

Vasos was obviously in need of strong coffee to sober him up before taking the wheel so I walked the gangplank once more, crossing the road to buy three takeout coffees from the nearest café. By the time I returned Vasos was exiting the toilet, a trace of scented soap almost disguising the permanent aroma of sweat. Grabbing the coffee he thanked me with a beaming smile before heading back to the wheelhouse to dress in the filthy clothes he'd earlier discarded. I hoped he would at least refrain from adding a splash of ouzo to his coffee until we'd cleared the harbour.

Within minutes Vasos emerged from the wheelhouse, greedily chomping down on a rather stale spinach pie that looked as though it was well past its expiry date, probably retrieved from under the pile of manky towels that served as his blanket. Noticing the first eager looking tourists heading towards the boat I grabbed the spinach pie from Vasos' grasp and hurriedly tossed it overboard. The tour company operated a very strict 'no food on the boat' policy and I could hardly be expected to rigorously police it if the Captain was spotted blatantly breaking the rules.

The tour company is hot on the no food rule, claiming food is a pollutant. However I rather fancy food is actually banned because the company earn a percentage commission on the tourist spend at the taverna we moor at for lunch. Enforcing the rule by summarily confiscating any food smuggled on board is the most onerous part of my job, but if I fail to implement it I risk Tiffany dragging me over the coals in the most condescending manner. The humiliation of being yelled at by a jumped-up twenty-something is not an experience I wish to repeat.

Chapter 14

Turning Ouzo into Water

I may have exaggerated just a tad when I said that Vasos doesn't speak a single word of English. His mastery of English vocabulary actually comprises exactly nine words, though it is decidedly questionable if he really understands the meaning of yes, no, hello, good, beautiful, towel, and I love you, since he scatters them with indiscriminate abandon. He appears to be under the impression that the word towel translates to let me rub you down, and he drops hello as both hello and goodbye, obviously under the delusion that the word is as interchangeable as the Greek word *yassas*. He always garners some amused looks when he bids hello to the tourists at the end of a boat trip, a characteristic cheery grin on his face as he bellows the word.

Being a very gregarious type with a constantly chirpy disposition, Vasos likes to stand beside me on the gangplank when I greet the tourists walking the plank for the lazy day cruise, ever optimistic that he can work his charm on a willing woman. As I ticked the names of the arrivals off against my list, Vasos extended a helpful hand to the ladies, careful they didn't plunge from the gangplank into the water, greeting them with a blustery "Hell-O," each syllable of the word over accentuated in typical Greek style.

There were the inevitable delays during boarding; a passenger wanting confirmation that she had been marked down for the vegetarian lunch option, another one wanting reassurance there were no sudden storms forecast. All the while Vasos stood firm beside me, selectively kissing or shaking hands, or slobbering and bone crushing depending on one's view, and booming "Hello, yes, good, hello beautiful." Thumping his chest with a stubby finger he introduced himself, saying "*Kapetanios*, good, good."

It was still too early in the day for Vasos to launch the full force of his charm offensive on any likely looking women, or declare his love to a random tourist. I was yet to observe Vasos have any success with the ladies, though they usually let him down gently, amused by his harmless and happy-go-lucky approach. At least I didn't have to stop any loose types throwing themselves at Vasos as I did with Sakis, the boat captain not exactly making the cut as the Greek god material that romantic holiday dreams are made of. Since I genuinely like Vasos I keep my fingers crossed that one day a woman lacking any olfactory senses may stumble on board and fall into his arms.

The day's group comprised mainly English tourists, all excited and eager to lift anchor and cruise the clear blue sea. Whilst Vasos went off to coax the engine into life, I gathered my charges to introduce myself and give them the spiel, filling them in on the day's itinerary and reeling off the rules: absolutely no food on board, no running, no tripping the decks in high heels, and no stuffing paper down the toilet.

Demonstrating a complete lack of interest a handful of sun worshippers disappeared to the upper deck to bag the best spots to sprawl out on their towels and top up their tans, whilst the more culturally minded day trippers keenly absorbed the information I imparted about the day's programme. I explained that we would cruise along at a gentle pace, following the coast line, and that I would be on hand to point out such fascinating landmarks as old pirate caves and a lighthouse.

The scheduled programme included dropping anchor for a pre-lunch swim. I took the opportunity to caution any inexperienced swimmers amongst the group against attempting to dive from the upper deck, pointing out that a badly executed dive could turn into a humiliating belly flop resulting in unsightly contusions and abdominal injuries. Considering how close I'd come to belly flopping from the diving board the previous day, I was careful to put an especial stress on this warning. I also underscored the importance of not hogging the ladder, and explained that a number of swimming floats and inflatable noodles would be made available for those venturing into the water. Following the swim stop we would cruise to a picturesque fishing village for a taverna lunch of chicken souvlaki or stuffed vegetables, preferences already ticked off at the time of booking. Finally on the return trip we would once again drop anchor, this time to swim with a watermelon. With the day's programme spelled out I encouraged the tourists to find a comfortable spot, reminding them to slap on the sunscreen and wear a hat.

"It sounds like a lovely day out," Mrs Bagshaw said.

"I'm sure you'll enjoy it," I replied, rather perturbed to hear Mr Conley chuntering away behind me to his wife, saying, "These reps don't half go on, this chap must love the sound of his own voice. We knew all that from the leaflet."

"There's no need to be rude about it dear, he's just doing his job. Not everyone reads all the blumpf," Mrs Conley said.

"Jobsworth more like," Mr Conley harrumphed, pulling his hat down over his eyes and settling down on the wooden bench. "This is a bit uncomfy, pass me that towel to sit on, I don't want to get splinters in my backside."

Sighing deeply his wife passed him a towel before reaching into her beach bag to extract a paperback copy of the latest airport bestseller. I made a mental leap, imagining one day Mrs Conley would relax on deck with her nose buried in my own bestseller, too fascinated by the Bucket saga to even notice the stunning Greek backdrop on offer. Of course if I wished to preserve my anonymity I would need to keep schtum about owning up to my authorship.

Moving on I started to make my rounds, exchanging pleasantries with the tourists and answering any questions they had. Before climbing up to the upper deck I took a moment to lean over the railings, inhaling the fresh sea air, the boat's onward motion through the water throwing up a fine mist that looked invitingly cool in the heat. Sami shuffled along to stand beside me. Naturally I didn't expect a reply from my weather-beaten silent companion when I observed it was a beautiful day, *"mia omorfi imera,"* but he lifted his head in acknowledgment, before scuttling off, dragging the mop behind him.

Climbing aloft I could almost smell the aroma of burning skin as newly arrived in Greece tourists exposed their delicate white flesh to the rays of the unforgiving sun. Instead of gradually exposing limbs slathered in protective factor fifty, this current contingent of sunbathers seemed to welcome the burn on their oil slicked skin. I predicted there would be some painful and peeling red bodies by evening.

Reflecting that the typical British holiday-maker seemed oblivious to the health and safety aspects of overdoing the sun, I prudently bit my tongue. I recalled that after harping on about safe sunbathing precautions during my first boat rodeo as a rep, I'd been marked down on the customer satisfaction survey, with one holidaymaker scribbling in the comments section that I was an interfering health and safety killjoy. The more pragmatic approach was to leave them to it and let them slowly roast.

Moving down from the upper deck I stepped into the wheel house to see how Vasos was doing; our little chats really helped to improve my Greek language skills. "*Pos paei?*" I said, asking how things were going. "Good," Vasos replied, demonstrating his masterful command of English before reverting to Greek to ask how things were with me. "*Kai eseis? Thelis ouzo?*"

Tapping my watch to indicate it was well before noon, I declined his offer of a morning tipple.

"*Pigaino toualeta.*" Vasos indicated I should take charge of the wheel whilst he went to the toilet, a rash state of affairs considering I wasn't trained to handle any nautical emergencies. Fortunately the sea before me was calm and there were no other boats on the horizon for me to worry about colliding with.

As soon as Vasos exited the wheel house I took the opportunity to sniff his bottle of water.

As I suspected it was practically neat ouzo. Substituting the bottle for a new bottle of actual water I sidled past Vasos the moment he returned, tipping the fiery contents over the side of the vessel; it wouldn't do to have Vasos arrested for being drunk in charge of a pleasure cruise. Fortunately he failed to notice my sleight of hand, being otherwise distracted.

"Victor, beautiful, beautiful, good yes," he shouted excitedly, grabbing hold of my arm and pointing to the upper sun deck that backed onto the wheel house. I didn't know where to look, mortified at the sight of a middle aged woman shamelessly flaunting her ample topless bosom. Clearly not sharing my embarrassed restraint, Vasos shouted "I love you," his eyes bulging out of his head on stalks as he pantomimed blowing kisses. Unable to hear him over the roar of the engines the woman gave him a cheery wave, before settling down on her stomach to work on turning her back into a slab of raw meat.

Returning to the main deck I pretended not to notice Mr Conley chomping away on a flaky pie. He struck me as the obstreperous type who would make a scene if I attempted to confiscate his snack. Strolling around the deck with a smile to encourage conversation I was glad to stop and pass the time with Roger and Tillie Mason, an elderly couple who told me they'd signed up for the day cruise to test their sea legs as they quite fancied booking a cruise around the Greek islands for their next vacation.

"Have you ever done a Greek island cruise Victor?" Tillie asked.

"No, a cruising holiday is something that was never on our bucket list," I admitted. Although it was something Marigold and I had occasionally discussed, we had ruled cruising out. Even before meeting Harold and Joan we had a horror of being stuck in confined proximity with the likes of them.

"Silly of me to ask really," Tillie said. "With you living over here you don't need to go on vacation; every day must be a holiday."

"Well not quite, I'm actually working today," I pointed out.

"You can hardly count swanning about on the Med as work," Roger snorted. "You ought to try working for the council for a living, now that's real work.

"I take it you worked for the council then..."

"Indeed, before I retired I was a labour inspector, visiting work premises to ensure they complied with safety legislation. It was no picnic

I can tell you, there's many an employer happy to cut corners and jeopardise the safety of their workers."

"I can imagine, I was a public health inspector before moving to Greece. Some of the establishments I visited would have been responsible for poisoning half of Manchester with their filthy practices if I hadn't been on the ball."

"I can see why you jacked it in for a cushy job over here," Mark said.

"You'd have had a field day in Greece with your inspections," I said. "I've never once seen a builder in a hard hat in spite of stringent EU regulations."

Our conversation was interrupted by Vasos screeching my name. "Please excuse me, I think I hear the *Kapetanios* calling."

"Perhaps we can catch up over lunch," Roger suggested. "You can fill me in on the type of safety ordinances the Greeks breach."

"Roger, you're on holiday, forget about work," Millie said. "Can you believe he's been retired for over fourteen years, yet he's still obsessed with safety violations?"

"It's a hard habit to break," I replied, wondering if I would still be obsessed with hygiene standards after fourteen years of retirement.

BUCKET TO GREECE (VOL. 4)

When I returned to the wheelhouse Vasos thrust his bottle of water under my nose, telling me to try it because it tasted funny. After blatantly fibbing and assuring him that the water in his bottle was definitely ouzo, he scratched his head. I must have put on a convincing performance because he raised his bottle, gulping back the contents with obvious relish before pronouncing it "good." It must have hit the spot as Vasos gave me the thumbs up before declaring, "I love you Victor." Sami clanked into the wheelhouse, dragging his mop and bucket. Catching his eye Vasos declared "I love you Sami." I couldn't help liking the *Kapetanios.* Despite his lack of personal hygiene he was certainly a chirpy character.

Chapter 15

Wondrous Delight

As we cruised by the natural openings in the cliff face Vasos slowed the boat down. The day trippers looked on with interest, appreciating the magnificent sight, entranceways appearing as forbidding portals to dark, dank secret places of mythical allure set into craggy and towering rocks. I painted a picture to my captive audience of ancient hollowed out fissures, perhaps leading into gloomy impenetrable subterranean spaces, uninviting yet paradoxically invitingly cool on such a clear hot day. The history buffs amongst my charges were fascinated as I entertained them with stories about smugglers' coves; and of pirates hiding their plundered treasures in these secret spots.

I recalled Marigold and I venturing into a cave hollowed into the hillside in the neighbouring village of Nektar, the slimy stones a myriad of colours near to the entrance, dark and foreboding further in, the silence only broken by the persistent drip-drip of water. We decided against exploring further because Marigold was terrified there may be bats waiting to pounce on her hair, and the ground was nothing but a squelchy mess of cow dung, a local farmer having made use of the cave for his apparently flatulent herd. Still I digress from the caves at hand: I was heartened that my talk elicited so much interest in these natural phenomena since it demonstrated that not everyone on board was a sun worshipping Philistine.

Those disappointed that the Pegasus trip did not allow for an exploration of the caves were pleased by my recommendation that they sign up for a guided tour of the Caves of Diros, led by Cynthia. The tour offers the opportunity to glide by narrow boats through an impressive flooded cave complex, rich in dramatic formations of stalagmites. I jotted down the names of those eager to visit Diros; if they committed to the tour I planned to extort a percentage of the commission from my soon-to-be sister-in-law.

A short time later Sami dropped anchor and I invited everyone to take a dip and cool off in the crystal clear water. Overly hot from standing around in the heat, I envied the trippers opportunity to swim, but frolicking around in the sea was frowned upon in my official capacity as rep. Instead I was tasked with the obligation of ensuring no one drowned. I wasn't expected to serve as an actual lifeguard, but rather as lookout, keeping my eyes peeled for signs of anyone in distress. A quick blow on my whistle would summon *Kapetanios* Vasos and his trusty sidekick who would leap to the rescue. It was very fortunate that Sami's muteness wasn't accompanied by deafness or he would never hear the blast of the whistle.

Vasos and I huddled close to the top of the ladder, offering helping hands to ascending swimmers, Vasos nudging me out of his way if any female not resembling the back of a bus put a foot on the rungs. The cheery way he extended a hand whilst saying "hello beautiful towel," his eyes fixated on their bosoms, tended to elicit a smiling response, negating any impression of peeping Tom perviness. Our close proximity to the ladder at least offered the chance to cool off when fearless tourists leapt into the water from the upper deck, the eruption of water inevitably splashing us.

Almost everyone on board was delighted to indulge in a dip. Even though Mrs Conley voiced that she wasn't a particularly strong swimmer and hated to be out of her depth in the water, she managed to prise her nose out of the bestseller she'd been immersed in all morning and tentatively make her way down the ladder. Once in the water she made a grab for the inflated noodle I threw down for her to cling onto. Mr Conley failed to notice her absence, continuing to snooze on in the sunlight, his legs beginning to turn an interesting shade of red, though at least his bald pate was protected by a sunhat.

"You should come in the water Victor, it's just lovely," Tillie Mason called up.

"I wish I could, but I'm working you know," I reminded her before heading into the wheelhouse to grab my bottle of sunscreen for a top up. Rubbing the lotion into my nose I had a bird eye's view of the deck. Looking down I witnessed an eruption of water cascading over the side of the boat, rudely disturbing Mr Conley from his slumber. "What the dickens..." he roared, before looking round to discover the deck was empty. Not wishing to be on the receiving end of his surly temper I stayed out of view, watching as he caught sight of Sami and called out, "Have we stopped for lunch already?"

Unfortunately Sami was not only incapable of answering, but even of understanding the question. Muttering "how bloody rude," Mr Conley walked over towards Vasos. "Hey, you're in charge, why did no one tell me we'd stopped, have I missed lunch?"

"Good hello," Vasos replied, unable to understand a word.

"I said have we stopped for lunch?" Mr Conley said in raised voice, falling into the stereotypical tradition of Brits speaking very loudly in the belief that it will make ignorant foreigners suddenly understand them.

"Yes," Vasos responded, presumably thinking the use of the English word would stop the Englishman shouting at him.

"Yes, then why did no one tell me?" Mr Conley bellowed.

"*Ti?*" Vasos replied, cocking his head to one side, clueless he was creating a passable impression of Manuel, the permanently confused Spanish waiter in Fawlty Towers.

"Ti. What is this ti? Speak English man. I demand to know why no one told me the boat had stopped. What have you done with my wife?"

"Yes, beautiful," Vasos shouted, presumably taking a stab that one of the other words in his immense English vocabulary would calm the obstreperous tourist down.

"Beautiful, are you trying to poke fun at my wife just because she's no oil painting?" Mr Conley enunciated loudly and slowly, a threatening scowl on his face.

"*Victor, ella edo. Victor ella,*" Vasos bellowed.

"*Erchomai,*" I replied, hurrying over to diffuse the situation before it turned nasty. "We anchored up for a swim Mr Conley. Mrs Conley is in the water."

"Then why didn't this blasted idiot say so?" Mr Conley demanded, finally looking down to the water and spotting his wife floating along with the noodle, oblivious to her husband's tantrum.

"I'm afraid the *Kapetanios* doesn't speak any English," I explained.

"He doesn't speak English," Mr Conley parroted.

"Well he is Greek, and we are in Greece," I pointed out, adding "I always try to put myself in Greek shoes. If a Greek was to turn up in England he wouldn't expect all and sundry to understand him, and speaking louder wouldn't help."

"I suppose not, I never thought of it like that. It's a good thing you're along to translate. Ah well, at least I haven't missed lunch," Mr Conley said, moseying back to his bench seat and sticking his nose in his wife's bestseller. I hazarded a guess that his newly red complexion was down to embarrassment rather than too much sun. Glancing up he caught my eye and nodded in a friendly fashion, perhaps reflecting he'd made a bit of an ass of himself over nothing. Struck by his sudden contemplative air I wandered over and offered him my bottle of sunscreen. "Your legs could do with a bit of this or you'll suffer later."

"Very decent of you," Mr Conley acknowledged.

With everyone back on board and towelled off, I did a quick head count. It wouldn't do to leave anyone behind in the water; Tiffany took a very dim view of us losing tourists. Vasos chartered Pegasus' course towards our lunchtime destination, the sea still amazingly calm as we cruised with little sign of a breeze to counter the heat. With my duties discharged until we disembarked for lunch I strolled to the bow to catch a quiet moment. It was a truly glorious day and I relished being out on the water. Suddenly a movement to the right of the boat caught my eye. It was too far in the distance for me to discern clearly, but whatever it was appeared to be heading straight towards us. For a brief moment I pondered the possibility that we had come across a latter day Sami needing rescuing from the sea. The moment passed and I could clearly discern figures in the water.

"Vaso delfinia," I yelled at the top of my lungs. Realising the sound of the engine drowned out my excited call I rushed back to the main deck, alerting everyone that we were about to be joined by a pod of dolphins. Calling up to Vasos I shouted *"Vaso, delfinia sta dexia."* Grabbing his binoculars Vasos sighted the pod and slowed the boat so that everyone could enjoy the impromptu performance by the magnificent aquatic creatures playfully arching their backs and jumping across the surface of the water.

Every single person on board rushed to starboard, even the sunbathers prising themselves off their towels, cameras poised to capture the moment. For one fleeting moment I worried the sheer weight of people leaning over the starboard railings would tip the boat over. The dolphins provided incredibly captivating spontaneous entertainment for fifteen minutes before turning tail, leaving the general mood on board one of wondrous delight.

Pegasus continued onwards towards our lunch-time destination, a tiny picturesque fishing village boasting a handful of sea side tavernas, an idyllically quiet spot with a pebble beach running into shallow waters. Killing the engine Vasos rushed to take his spot on the gangplank, bidding hello to the tourists as he extended a hand to help them onto dry land. Returning my bottle of sun screen Mr Conley asked me what the Greek word for hello was and I explained that *yassas* served as both hello and goodbye. When he drew level with Vasos he said "*Yassas* Captain," even managing to take it in his stride when Vasos replied "beautiful hello."

I made a mental note to at least try to add some context to Vasos' limited English vocabulary. Although he had no interest in learning my language I could at least steer him away from the inappropriate habit of addressing men as beautiful. One of these days some random chap may get the wrong end of the stick. I would hate for Vasos to have his lights punched out by some fellow thinking that he'd been propositioned by the pungently eager Kapetanios.

Chapter 16

Swimming with Watermelons

F ollowing the fabulous dolphin display, nothing could disrupt the glorious collective mood of the day trippers. On occasion the scheduled lunch stops on the lazy day cruises could be a tad lacklustre, throwing together a mishmash of dull types not inclined to interact with strangers, casting wary looks at one another, forced to share the same table for lunch but never actually clicking. On other days a handful of miserable types grumbling about petty inconveniences could sap all the fun out of my trip.

Not so today, the pods magical performance having injected exuberance into the communal mood, imbuing my charges with an abundance of Greek *kefi*, laughter and chatter filling the air.

After ensuring the tourists were all seated at one of the two long tables allocated to our group, I had a discreet word with the waiter to make sure that Vasos was only served very dilute ouzo, before taking a seat next to the captain and Sami. The nautical pair was already tucking hungrily into bread and *tzatziki*, whilst the taverna staff passed round plates of chicken souvlaki or stuffed vegetables to our party. Once all the paying customers had a plate of delicious Greek food in front of them I tried to catch the waiter's eye since the three of us remained foodless.

"Perimene Victor, o filos mou fernei to fresko kalamari," Vasos said, telling me his friend the waiter was bringing us fresh squid. I was delighted to hear of this unexpected departure from our usual menu; it was beginning to get a bit repetitive eating chicken or stuffed courgettes week after week, particularly in light of the recent glut of said vegetable in my garden. The squid was instead a mouth-watering treat of tender tentacles, cooked to perfection without a hint of rubberiness.

Mrs Bagshaw, seated beside me, winced at the sight of my *kalamari*. "Oh bad luck, did they run out of chicken? I don't think I could bring myself to eat that." It suited me to have her assume that we'd been served some sub-par replacement dish; it wouldn't do for the paying tourists to guess the crew had been given preferential treatment.

After polishing off his chicken souvlaki, Mr Conley, seated opposite the captain, attempted to engage him in conversation, having obviously taken my earlier words to heart. Deliberately thumping his own chest in a passable impression of Tarzan he slowly and clearly said "Me Brian. I am sixty." Mrs Conley lifted her head out of her paperback for long enough to roll her eyes at her husband's out of character behaviour. Vasos stared at Mr Conley long and hard before the light bulb switched on. Shaking his head in agreement and thumping his own chest, he said "Me Kapetanios, me towel."

Rather baffled by this response Mr Conley chewed on his lower lip in confusion before passing Vasos a paper napkin, helpfully supplying the nearest thing to the aforementioned towel. Fixing his eye on me Mr Conley said, "I'm not sure if he understood me. Can you help out?"

"Of course," I replied. Turning to Vasos I told him *"To onoma tou einai Brian, einai exinda."*

"Echei mia omorfi gynaika, isos na kolymoiso mazi tis argotera," Vasos replied.

Having no intention of telling the English man that Vasos had said that Mr Conley had a beautiful wife and perhaps he would swim with her later, I deliberately mistranslated. "He says it's a pleasure to meet you."

Before I could be called upon for anymore quick-on–my-feet evasive translating, I was dragged to one side by Roger Mason.

"I can't get over the way these Greeks tear round on their motorcycles without wearing crash helmets, surely they must be flouting the law?"

"It's certainly a bit dare-devilish," I agreed. "However I think if they carry the crash helmet on their person they aren't technically breaking the law."

Mr Mason appeared confused by my answer so I expanded my explanation. "If they have the helmet over one arm then technically they are wearing it on their person, thus complying with the law."

"Only yesterday I spotted a helmetless motor-cyclist with three passengers all crammed on…"

"It's amazing how many one can get onto a motorcycle with a bit of ingenuity," I agreed. It was not that out of the ordinary to spot a family of five and the family goat all squashed onto one ropey looking moped.

Out of the corner of my eye I spotted Vasos heading off in the direction of the bar. Excusing myself I chased after the captain, hoping to intercept him before he could down a large tumbler of ouzo. "*Pou pas Vaso*?" I asked, enquiring where he was off to, only to feel rather foolish when he informed me he was on his way to the toilet.

As I lurked outside the toilet with the express intention of ensuring Vasos' lunchtime stop remained alcohol free, I was cornered by another chatty tourist from our boat party who was curious about my decision to retire to a foreign country. I became so caught up in our conversation, telling Mrs Andrews all about our efforts to integrate into the local community, that Vasos managed to sneak by me and down a large ouzo before I could stop him. Asking Mrs Andrews to excuse me I dashed off in hot pursuit of Vasos, catching up with him just as he threw an arm around Mrs Foot's shoulder, testing out his new chat up line, "Me Brian, I am sixty."

"You don't look it, I'd have guessed you were

in your mid-fifties," Mrs Foot replied genially, clueless the captain was clueless to the meaning of the English words he had just uttered.

"Towel good," Vasos said. Grabbing his arm I steered him back to the boat, asking the waiter to make him a strong *Ellinkos*. We still had another half-hour before it was time to cast off the anchor, plenty of time for Vasos to down a strong Greek coffee.

With Vasos safely back on the boat and out of random chat up range, I decided to take a leisurely stroll around the small charming harbour before re-boarding. A number of colourful wooden fishing boats were moored, mostly empty since most of the fishermen had headed home after bringing in their morning catch. A solitary fisherman was tidying his nets, his gnarled fingers moving at speed as he untangled the knots. I did a double take, suddenly noticing the name painted on the side of his boat was *Katifes*: Marigold.

Calling out to him I said *"Katifes. To onoma tis gynaika mou einei Katifes."* It wasn't strictly true of course since Marigold is actually my wife's pseudonym, fondly adopted to preserve her anonymity amidst these pages.

"Oraio onama," a beautiful name, the fisher-

man called out, tipping his cap.

With the *kalamari* walked off I rounded up my charges ready to set sail on our return journey. As Vasos greeted the returning passengers he wowed them with his newly acquired word sixty, scattering it amid his random use of hello, towel and beautiful. I must say it was strangely well received by the tourists who shook his hand, proclaiming he was a real character.

Everyone relaxed in the sunshine as we cruised back down the coast, the rising temperature making all on board eager to get back in the water on our scheduled afternoon stop to swim with the watermelon. Since we were more than forty on board Sami would actually be chucking two watermelons in the sea, a sure fire way of cooling the fresh fruit down before he carved it into slices to be shared out amongst everyone.

As soon as the anchor was dropped Vasos flopped down in the wheelhouse for an afternoon siesta, instructing me not to wake him unless there was an emergency. With Sami diving after the watermelons he tossed into the water, I was left as the sole lookout, obliged to explain "I'm afraid he's a mute," each time someone ascended the ladder complaining the captain's sidekick had ignored their questions asking if it was a Greek tradition to swim with a watermelon, or if any buoyant fruit would do. Feeling decidedly envious of the holidaymakers swimming below me I made a mental note to strip off my uniform and dive in once we returned to the harbour, having taken the precaution of stuffing a pair of freshly ironed swim shorts into my work satchel.

Sami struggling to keep hold of the two large melons as he climbed back on-board was my cue to round up my sea-frolicking charges, using the promise of freshly chilled watermelon as a lure. Even those reluctant to leave the water couldn't resist the temptation of the deliciously juicy red fruit, gathering round to watch Sami wield an over-sized knife, cutting the melon with such precision that all the slices were of exact equal size. I made a mental note to keep on the good side of Sami: the way he wielded the knife put me in mind of Frenk slashing Tarek with his Kosovan *Rugovo spathi*.

Kicking Vasos awake I hoped he wouldn't wander the deck miming that he was happy to lick the juice off a melon splattered sticky tourist woman as he'd done on the previous trip. Unfortunately the fruit proved a magnet, attracting a veritable swarm of wasps, sending half-a-dozen of the more squeamish tourists running down into the hold screaming in terror.

As Vasos steered the boat back to our embarkation point he passed me a paper detailing the coming week's schedule with the tour company. In addition to the lazy day cruises his schedule generally included trips down to the Caves of Diros, a lazy day cruise with a beach barbecue, and moonlight cruises; he also occasionally hired the boat out for private charters on days when the tour company didn't need his services. Pointing to a date on the schedule for Thursday week, Vasos asked me if I'd be repping that trip, expressing his hope that I would be, assuring me that I was his favourite rep and he regarded me as a foreign brother. To emphasise the point he broke into English, proclaiming "I love you Victor."

Touched that I was his favourite rep, I nevertheless had to break the bad news that he would need to do without me the following Thursday since I had the day booked off for Cynthia's...

Vasos interrupted me before I could finish my sentence.

"*I Cynthia einai i agapimeni mou.*" Vasos' declaration that Cynthia was his favourite surprised me in light of his very recent declaration that I held that favoured position. Obviously the man was fickle. "*I Cynthia echei gyalisteria mallia, myrizei oraia,*" Vasos added, declaring that Cynthia had glossy hair that smelled good. Grabbing a towel he inhaled its pungent stench, a gesture I guessed was meant to mimic his desire to bury his nose in Cynthia's glossy locks.

With Vasos otherwise engaged with the towel I finally managed to finish telling him why I wouldn't be repping the following Thursday, explaining I would be attending Cynthia's wedding.

Vasos nearly keeled over in shock, proclaiming he had no idea that the beautiful Cynthia was about to be married. He found it impossible to believe that she hadn't mentioned this life-changing event to him on one of their trips to Diros. Mulling over the prospect of Cynthia's wedding Vasos suddenly exclaimed that it was odd that she hadn't invited him, especially since I would be attending. I explained that the wedding was only a small affair and I was on the guest list because Cynthia was marrying my brother-in-law, so it was a family affair.

It transpired that Vasos had plenty to say on the matter, for once not bothering to speak slow and precise Greek for my benefit, not caring if I understood him. I hazarded a guess that the gist of his rant centred on either Cynthia turning down his own marriage proposal, or not inviting him to the wedding: my translating skills weren't up to the job of definitively plumping for one scenario over the other. It was true that Vasos did have a habit of dropping random marriage proposals, but Cynthia had never mentioned receiving one. Fortunately Vasos hadn't yet discovered how to propose marriage in English, sparing myriads of tourist women the ordeal of turning him down.

As Vasos continued his rant I was unwilling to admit I was clueless to half of what he was saying. In the hope of calming him down I simply humoured him by agreeing with whatever he said, puncturing his rant with the occasional *"nai, nai,"* as he became louder and more excitable. When he finally paused for breath, taking his hands off the wheel to plant them firmly on my cheeks and deposit a kiss on my forehead, I began to wonder what on earth I had said yes to that had calmed him down and put a smile on his face. I had a sinking feeling that he may be under the impression I'd just invited him to the wedding. Since I couldn't be sure I was left in two minds whether I should mention anything to Cynthia unless he actually gate-crashed her wedding.

"Good yes," Vasos said to me as we stood side by side on the gangplank offering steadying hands to the departing tourists.

"*Poli kali mera,*" I replied, confirming it had been a very good day.

"Hell-O, Hell-O," Vasos shouted, bidding farewell to the happy day trippers and kissing Mrs Foot's hand when she told him "It's been such a wonderful trip Captain Brian."

Mr Conley paused to shake the captain's hand firmly, generously distributing five euro notes to myself, Sami and Vasos. He looked rather taken aback for a moment when Vasos accepted his tip cheerily, saying "sixty." Fortunately Vasos also randomly dropped the world towel, convincing Mr Conley that the captain was simply spewing odd English words rather than implying the five euro tip should be rounded up to sixty.

Reflecting that I could comfortably expect to receive all round high scores on that day's customer satisfaction survey I paddled into the onboard toilet to change into my swim shorts. A refreshing dip would be a wonderful end to a satisfying day's repping.

Chapter 17

Tesco Pickles

Marigold was relaxing on the balcony when I returned home, the sun highlighting the lovely Titian glow of her hair. Sinking into the chair beside her I recalled that she had spent the afternoon having her roots touched up in Athena's kitchen, and duly complimented her hair.

"It's no picnic having one's head plastic wrapped in this heat. Did you have a nice day out on the boat dear?"

"Excellent, but I *was* working you know."

"If that's what you call cruising round on the Med," Marigold scoffed, seemingly oblivious that with travel time included I had put in a ten-hour day. "Doreen popped in for coffee this morning. She seemed to think it all went swimmingly yesterday evening. She even remarked that you won't be so quick to drop scurrilous slurs about her cooking in future seeing as you polished off every morsel of the chicken parmesan."

"Hmm," I said noncommittally, hoping that Milton and Edna's stomachs had survived their dodgy doggy-bag lunch.

"I had the most peculiar conversation with Doreen, very bizarre," Marigold continued. "She'd got it into her head that we have a surfeit of kittens and should donate one to Spiros' sickly uncle Leo as an emotional support animal. I was quite surprised that she seemed so concerned about him, after all it was the first time she'd met him. Still I can't imagine how she came up with such a crazy notion, I said to her you can't expect us to just go around giving away kittens to all and sundry, Clawsome is very attached to her offspring and they're part of our family."

"That's not strictly true, Clawsome has never demonstrated even a soupcon of motherly instincts towards her kittens, and they do tend to get under our feet," I pointed out.

"How can you be so callous?" Marigold accused.

"I'm afraid it comes naturally where the devil spawn of Cynthia's mutant rapist Tom and your imported Clawsome are concerned."

Sticking an aggrieved expression on her face Marigold reminded me, "They do have names, you know? How would you feel if the cats went around talking about that tall man instead of referring to you by name?"

Ignoring her preposterous reasoning I said, "Marigold, I will never understand what possessed you to give those creatures such ridiculous names. I've never heard of anything as asinine as naming a pet after a supermarket."

"Finishing off the last jar of Tesco pickles made me nostalgic. That reminds me, we must ask Benjamin to smuggle some more silver skins over when he visits. Perhaps I'll ask him to bring a kitten teething ring too, I'm a tad worried about Tesco's teeth," Marigold said.

"Tesco's teeth looked fine to me when it had that vole clamped between them last week. Anyway I don't recall you being so keen on your precious kitten when it deposited its live prey in the kitchen, you were balanced on top of the kitchen table for a good ten minutes. I was worried you'd fall off and do yourself an injury," I retorted.

"You know how voles make me squeamish. They remind me of that creepy hamster Benjamin kept in his bedroom as a child. I can still picture his science teacher's face when she discovered Benjamin had used his pet as the centrepiece of that disastrous experiment; I was so embarrassed," Marigold winced. "Anyway we should be vole free in future. I've upped Tesco's and Pickle's food allowance so that they won't have the urge to hunt."

"The urge to hunt is ingrained because they have free rein to roam. You can hardly expect the spawn of Kouneli to be cossetted domestics content to chow down on Whiskas like the imports," I said. "And if Tesco takes after its tomcatting father then in no time at all we can expect it to start indulging in ravaging sprees, terrorising every cat in the village. The neighbours are going to love us."

"We can have Tesco seen to before he gets the urge to go calling on female felines," Marigold argued.

"So that's my repping wages accounted for, I may just as well cut out the middleman and tell

Tiffany to hand all my wages over to the veterinarian."

Climbing onto her high-horse, Marigold proclaimed, "Victor, you're not the only one who contributes, only this morning I sold half-a-dozen newly laid eggs to Doreen." My wife completely disregarded the fact that she'd never actually ventured into the chicken coop due to the smell. "Now hush, here's Cynthia returning from her trip to Vathia, we don't want her to catch us bickering."

"Perish the thought," I retorted, determined to have the last word.

"Did you have a nice day out, dear?" Marigold asked Cynthia. My soon-to-be sister in law appeared rather dishevelled and over-heated as she joined us on the balcony, her new modacrylic uniform looking as though it had been put through the wringer.

"I *was* working, you know," Cynthia replied wearily. "I'd have been home an hour ago if some strange chap from Macclesfield hadn't wandered off when it was time to re-board the coach. I had to go searching for him in the ruined buildings; some of them haven't had a good sweeping out for years." As if to emphasise the point Cynthia retrieved a dusty looking cobweb from the depths of her cleavage. I cringed in disgust as she carelessly wiped it off on the tea-towel; the woman was becoming decidedly lax lately when it came to hygiene standards. "I was very tempted to leave Macclesfield man behind, but Sakis didn't dare risk Tiffany's wrath."

"Well we all know how Tiffany frowns on us losing tourists," I said.

"I know, but it's ridiculous how we allow a jumped up twenty-something to call the shots. I'm very tempted to put in for a promotion once the wedding's out of the way. It might be worth the extra paperwork to have Tiffany answering to me for a change. How did you get on with the cruise Victor?"

"It was an excellent day. I wouldn't be at all surprised if some of my holidaymakers leave glowing reviews on that new holiday review site," I boasted.

"Trip Advisor? I think that's just a passing fad, I don't see it taking off," Cynthia said.

"I expect you're right. By the way, how come you didn't mention to the *Kapetanios* that you are getting married next week? It took him completely by surprise."

"Oh you know what Vasos is like, forever declaring his love and proposing marriage," Cynthia said, rolling her eyes.

"I'm not sure he's strictly serious," I said.

"I should hope not, the man is clearly deluded if he even remotely thinks he's in with a chance, someone really should introduce him to the concept of deodorant. I prefer to keep his ardent attentions at arm's length by not divulging personal details of my private life."

"Perhaps he wouldn't keep proposing if you told him you had a fiancé," I suggested, imagining Vasos' unwanted attentions could feel a tad relentless to any woman on the receiving end. I endured his random kisses with good grace, confident he wasn't going to follow up by asking me out on a date.

"It's easier to just fob him off by telling him that I'm washing my hair or that the cat is sickly. It may only encourage him if he thought there was competition," Cynthia said.

"Well you certainly managed to keep Spiros at bay with that old chestnut that you were washing your hair," Marigold laughed.

"In Spiros' case I could never get past the smell of embalming fluid, but he was never as full on as Vasos," Cynthia admitted. "I'm so happy I met Barry. I do love the smell of sawdust, I find it very manly."

"Well you probably won't have to fight off Vasos' attentions in future. I let the cat out of the bag that you are marrying Barry next week, I can't see him propositioning a married woman," I said. Cynthia's eye roll made me suddenly doubtful as I recalled the way he'd fawned over Mrs Conley and Mrs Foot.

"Oh Victor, how could you be so dense, surely you know that will only encourage him. You must have noticed how Vasos loves the challenge of attempting to seduce married women," Cynthia cried.

"His seduction technique leaves a lot to be desired, I haven't seen any women melting into his arms at the mention of towels. I'm sure he'd propose to the watermelon if it had a pulse," I said

"Your captain certainly sounds like a character," Marigold laughed. Fluffing her newly touched up hair she added, "You must introduce me some time."

Sensing my wife was obviously in the market to add to her imagined cohort of Greek admirers I made a mental note to make more of an effort to shower her with attention, appreciating her desire to still have men find her attractive now she'd reached the stage of her life where she was completely reliant on stuff from a bottle to hide the grey.

"I've a feeling Vasos may gate-crash the wedding," I admitted, fully prepared for the full force of Cynthia's inevitable withering look.

Deftly changing the subject I asked my wife if she'd decided to join me later, babysitting Leontiades.

"I'm not sure yet. Have you any plans for this evening?" Marigold asked Cynthia.

"Yes, as soon as I've grabbed a quick shower I'm meeting Barry at Harold's place. We want to measure up and have a last look round before Barry signs the final papers with the notary tomorrow," Cynthia replied.

Attempting to hide her relief that Cynthia would be out of the house, Marigold decided "In that case I think I'll just have a quiet evening at home and enjoy a glass of wine on the roof terrace."

"It should be a spectacular sunset," I said.

"You don't mind babysitting alone, do you dear, after all you did volunteer?"

"I'm happy to do Spiros a favour. He's terribly smitten with Sampaguita and he deserves to find as much happiness as we have."

"Oh Victor, you'll make me blush," Marigold

gushed with not a hint of a flush. "Would you like me to make you a nice cheese sandwich before you go over to Leo's house?"

"No thanks, I'm fine. I shall just look in on the chickens and then jump in the shower before heading out," I said.

Chapter 18

The Return of the Sheep

Stepping into the garden to check on the chickens I reflected that Marigold's uninspiring cheese sandwich didn't deserve a look in since we were completely out of Tesco pickles to jazz it up. Spiros had telephoned earlier to confirm if I was still on for this evening. When I'd assured him it really was no trouble he told me that Sampaguita was insistent on preparing a special Filipino dish of pork adobo for my enjoyment. He assured me the traditional dish didn't incorporate any fried insects and I would feast on delectable tender belly pork, braised to perfection in garlic, vinegar and soy sauce.

Even though Spiros was generally reluctant to try any food that didn't replicate the Greek delights that his dear departed Granny had produced in her kitchen, he had become quite bold when it came to sampling foreign fare prepared by his fragrant Filipina flower. Spiros had even pretended to relish the Filipino dish of tipaklong, comprising fried grasshoppers, to get in her good graces. My mouth watered at the prospect of tucking into Sampaguita's pork adobo since I have an adventurous palate for exotic food prepared in hygienic conditions.

I was pleased to see Guzim hard at work in the garden, though I winced when I noticed he was using his bare hands to scrape chicken poop into a carrier bag. It appeared he was well on his way to cornering the market in selling fresh chicken waste as an organic fertiliser to gullible British ex-pats down on the coast, happy to spread our stinking droppings in their gardens. They appeared seemingly oblivious that a bag of age-dried goat manure could be had for a reasonable price from Lefteris' garden centre, minus the stench that inevitably came with fresh offerings. Since launching his burgeoning manure re-sale business Guzim had expanded beyond chicken and rabbit droppings, persuading Panos to part with the muck from his farm, for a cut of the profits.

Guzim was saving up for the bus fare home. His wife Luljeta was apparently keen for him to take a return trip to the homeland, Luljeta being eager to expand their family, impressed by the positive change in Guzim since the arrival of baby Fatos, named in honour of the questionably handsome Prime Minister of Albania. It appeared that Guzim felt a patriotic duty to single-handedly enlarge the population of Albania since there seemed little prospect of acquiring the necessary paperwork to bring his brood of four offspring to Greece. On the plus side though, his own recently acquired white paper practically protected him from deportation.

If, during a recent chat, I understood Guzim's guttural Greek correctly, it appeared he intended to knuckle down in Greece and make a modest fortune so that he could retire at a young age to the ramshackle rabbit farm in Albania. At some future date he planned to flog the stone shed at the bottom of my garden to another ambitious illegal immigrant. Upon hearing Guzim's plans I claimed first dibs on the stone shed; with a bit of imagination it could be transformed into an additional guest room. At the very least a vacant shed would spare my wife the indignity of accidentally confronting future generations of Albanians showering under the outside hosepipe.

Striding towards Guzim I made a mental note to avoid shaking his hand at all costs. Before he was even aware of my presence we were both disturbed by a loud scream, followed by angry shouting, emanating from the next door garden. Even before I had the chance to react, Guzim recklessly hurled himself over the garden wall, rushing to offer assistance to Kyria Maria, my eighty-year-old neighbour. Hurrying over to the wall I positioned myself to peer over and assess the threat, having no intention of rashly leaping into an unknown and potentially dangerous situation. I was amused to see my ancient neighbour attempting to shoo a stubbornly firm-footed sheep out of her garden, Guzim offering his assistance by clamping his chicken poop smeared hands firmly on either side of the immovable sheep's haunches and shoving for all he was worth.

Guzim pushed to no avail, the sheep appearing as stubborn as when it had impeded Marigold and my attempts to get past it the previous night.

V.D. BUCKET

Of course with one sheep looking much like another I was only hazarding a guess that it was indeed the same obstinate fearsome horned animal, but it looked suspiciously familiar. Unlike the general flock of more scrawny sheep that inhabited Meli, this one was fat, making it quite distinctive.

Without giving Guzim any advance warning the sheep suddenly moved sideways, leaving the hapless Albanian to fall flat on his face. With Guzim sprawled in the dirt the sheep mosied over towards Kyria Maria's peach tree. Standing on its hind legs it proceeded to nonchalantly chomp away at the tree's greenery, totally disregarding the old lady's feeble efforts to brush it away with a broom. I was quite impressed by its agility; being previously unaware sheep were capable of balancing on two legs.

"To provato einai..." I called over the wall to Maria, my sentence stopping abruptly short as I realised I was unable to complete 'the sheep is a nuisance' since I was clueless what the Greek word for nuisance was.

"To provato einai diavolos," Maria called back, finishing my sentence with the word devil, her attempts to brush the sheep away growing more desperate as the creature moved on from the

peach tree and started to munch it way through the chicory patch.

"To radiki einai to agapimeno mou yios," Maria exclaimed, frantic that the sheep was eating its way through her son's favourite vegetables. I made a mental note of Papas' Andreas favourite salad vegetable in case we should ever have him round for dinner and want to make a good impression by boiling up weeds.

I was still pondering the wisdom of clambering over the wall to lend a hand removing the sheep, when a piercing scream emanated from my house. Since the scream didn't sound like one of the usual panicked cries Marigold unleashes when some outside vermin ventures indoors and unnerves her, I immediately felt alarmed. I wasted no time in hot-footing it towards the house. Horrible images of an injured Marigold flitted through my mind as I dashed up the stairs, my heart racing. Rushing inside I exhaled in relief to see my beloved wife in one piece, looking decidedly sheepish as a towel clad Cynthia, still dripping from the shower, waved around a soggy piece of yellowed netting that stank to high heaven, in front of Marigold's face.

"What on earth is going on and what is that vile smell?" I demanded, nearly asphyxiated by the overpowering repugnant odour.

"It's ruined, ruined," Cynthia screeched like a banshee, Marigold practically cowering in mortification. "You shouldn't be allowed to have kittens if you can't control them."

Clueless what Marigold's kittens had actually done to earn this hysterical admonishment, I nevertheless considered it a bit rich coming from Cynthia of all people: Cynthia who failed so spectacularly in keeping her own repulsive mutant Tom from sneaking into people's homes on indiscriminate raping sprees.

Attempting to pull herself together Marigold said defensively, "I was just bringing you a glass of wine, I thought you would appreciate it when you got out of the shower."

"And it didn't occur to you to close the bedroom door behind you so that the kittens couldn't get in. Look at it, it's ruined, ruined," Cynthia cried, waving the soggy netting around in a manner that only served to waft the diabolical smell around. Even though I have never had the misfortune to encounter a skunk I imagine that they would smell like the offending material. Still it seemed that Cynthia was overreacting; there could be no excuse for speaking down to her hostess and soon-to-be sister-in-law in such a high-

handed manner, simply because a cat had presumably piddled on an old net curtain.

"I'm so sorry Cynthia, I can't apologise
enough. It was careless of me to leave the door
open..." Marigold began to say.

"Why on earth are you apologising to Cynthia after she spoke to you like that?" I interrupted, righteously indignant on my wife's behalf. "You have taken her into our home and this
is the sort of thanks you get."

"But Victor, Cynthia is entitled to be out-
raged. Tesco has ruined her wedding veil and it
is all my fault..."

"Her veil," I repeated, suddenly putting two
and two together and realising that what I'd presumed was a bit of tatty old net curtain was actually the cherished bridal veil that Cynthia had
splashed out a full month's wages on. I recalled
Marigold telling me that because of the heat Cynthia had opted against going full on puffy me-
ringue, instead choosing a chic and simple knee-
length summery white dress for her wedding, but
had splurged on a hideously expensive veil to
make her feel like a beautiful bride.

"Oh Cynthia, I can't tell you how sorry I am,
but I had no idea that Tesco would develop at
such a speed that his body is preparing for the

mating game and he'd start randomly spaying," Marigold said, her genuine remorse evident. Personally I still thought Cynthia's outburst unjustified considering there would have been no Tesco to spay her veil if she'd kept better control of her mutant tom in the first place.

Just then Barry arrived, chiding Cynthia for being late in meeting him at Harold's house. The poor chap was once again caught in the middle between his fiancé and his sister as Cynthia launched into a melodramatic account of how her precious veil came to be ruined. Sensing that Marigold was coming to the end of her patience and would be incapable of issuing grovelling apologies for much longer, I speedily stepped in with the perfect solution, suggesting the sensible course of action would be for us to find Tesco a new home before it could do any more damage.

"But we can take him up to the vet to be fixed," Marigold said.

"Well I don't know when, there's not a spare day in the calendar with the wedding coming up and our guests flying over on Sunday," I countered. "I've already committed to the new gastronomic tour…"

"And I am tied up tomorrow. I have a Greek lesson and then the ladies' sewing circle," Marigold said, realising a visit to the vet wasn't feasible. "Perhaps we could fix Cynthia's veil at our meeting, some of the Greek ladies are exceptionally skilled with a needle."

The four of us stared helplessly at the tatty netting. I had been so caught up in the stench of the soggy cloth that I'd failed to notice the kitten had torn it to shreds.

"It really would be best all round if we found a new home for Tesco," I urged again.

"I couldn't bear to part with Tesco unless it was to a loving home," Marigold hesitated, tears threatening to ruin her mascara.

"I have the perfect solution," I suggested. "Leontiades is in need of an emotional support animal. Only yesterday evening he demonstrated how inordinately fond he is of cats and the feeling appeared to be mutual. It proved practically impossible to prise Doreen's cat off his head. And of course if I take Tesco along to Leo's this evening I'm sure that Sampaguita would be happy for you to visit him anytime."

"I suppose so," Marigold reluctantly agreed. "But I worry Tesco will be lonely without his mother and brother."

"I can always take Pickles along with me too," I offered, hopeful of ridding the house of both kittens.

Looking at me appraisingly it was evident that Marigold's fighting spirit was returning. No longer dejectedly cowed, she snapped, "Don't push it Victor."

Out of the corner of one eye I caught sight of Cynthia's vile mutant cat Kouneli slinking out of the spare bedroom, the scrap of white veil trapped between its teeth indicating Tesco may in fact be a wrongly accused innocent party. Much as I would have loved to land Kouneli in it, I calculated we would soon be rid of the grotesque mutant when Barry and Cynthia moved out. Meanwhile the opportunity to rid the house of the vexatious kitten was too good to pass up.

Chapter 19

Spiros Walks on Water

A trace of disappointment flitted across Sampaguita's face as she greeted me on the doorstep of Leontiade's house. She had evidently expected to open the door to her devoted suitor.

"Oh Mr Bucket, do come in, I thought you were Spiros."

I didn't take offence at her hastily concealed lack of enthusiasm for my presence since her words were accompanied by a blush indicating that she was eager for her suitor to arrive to court her; a good sign I thought, hinting that Spiros' smitten feelings may well be reciprocated.

"Please no need to stand on ceremony, call me Victor."

"And how is Marigold? Your wife is so kind..."

"She's fine thank you, though a tad emotional to part with Tesco."

"Tesco?"

Reaching down I produced the cat basket containing the mischievous kitten that had been unjustly maligned for so wantonly ruining Cynthia's bridal veil. The stab of momentary guilt that I hadn't fessed up that the kitten was innocent, soon passed. It may be blameless on this occasion, but as the devil spawn of the vile mutant I was certain it would revel in wreaking havoc in the future, having surely inherited its tomcatting father's clearly warped genes.

Sampaguita's face melted in delight as she reached into the basket, immediately cradling the kitten as though it was her own new born. Showering the devil's spawn with indiscriminate kisses she gushed, "What an adorable kitten. I could just eat it up."

Fortunately the sparkle of happiness in her eyes led me to believe this was just a figure of speech and little Tesco was unlikely to end up in a traditional Filipino dish.

"Victor, I think you must be the very rare man to bring your pet with you, but I understand, it must be impossible for you to part with this beautiful kitten for even one minute."

Sampaguita had obviously got the wrong end of the stick; clueless I had no particular affection for cats she had mistakenly guessed I was bringing it along as a companion. Even though I must confess to a certain fondness for Marigold's imports, it didn't extend to Clawsome's litter.

"Actually little Tesco here is a gift for Leontiades, we thought it would be a comfort for him to have an emotional support animal now he's losing his faculties. Or course since the old chap isn't in the best of health the kitten's care would fall on you, so it's really your decision if Tesco has a new home here," I explained.

The soppy look on her face indicated the get-out clause was superfluous.

"Really, you wish to gift this adorable kitten to Leo. I have never heard of such kindness, such selfless generosity. But how can you bear to part with it?"

"We still have another one, Pickles, at home, plus two cats, three if you include that monstrous specimen that Cynthia has foisted upon us. It's not as if the kitten has any practical value like the chickens; really you'll be doing me in a favour in taking it off my hands."

Sampaguita's face expressed confusion; my casual attitude to dispensing with the kitten clearly marked me down as an unfeeling type with an irrational cat phobia. Still her delight at receiving the kitten apparently outweighed her sudden reservations about my rather questionable character. Burying her face in the fur on the kitten's belly she said, "You call it Tesco, I not hear this name before."

"I admit it was a bit of an odd choice to name the creature after a popular supermarket back in England, but it was Marigold's doing."

"I think I understand, Marigold could be homesick for the good English food. There is a friendly lizard in the courtyard, I call it Mik-Mik after my favourite Filipino childhood snack. It is impossible to find Mik-Mik in Greece. Even in Athens they not have the Reston's supermarket to buy the snack," Sampaguita said wistfully.

The arrival of Spiros in his hearse put an end to our chatter. The undertaker was obviously keen to make a good impression, having slathered on enough of his dead uncle's aftershave collection to effectively conceal the smell of embalming fluid. Presenting Sampaguita with a box of Lidl own brand chocolates he repeated a line he'd obviously picked up from some corny American movie, saying, "Sweets for my sweet."

Giggling appreciatively Sampaguita thrust Tesco under Spiros' nose, saying "And look at this adorable kitten that Victor has given me."

Spiros fired me a questioning look, as though I was having the audacity to move into his territory, attempting to outdo him by showering his fragrant Filipina flower with superior gifts.

"The kitten is a gift for your Uncle Leo actually. It was Doreen's idea, Leo seemed so taken with her pussy that she thought he would appreciate an emotional support animal," I hastily clarified.

A look of relief crossed Spiros' face when he realised I wasn't attempting to step on his toes by wooing Sampaguita with a cuddly kitten. Following Sampaguita into the house Spiros hissed to me, "The Sampaguita more like the kitten than the chocolate, I must to find her the kitten of her own."

"If you work your charm on Marigold you might be able to persuade her to part with Pickles," I suggested, sensing an opportunity to make the Bucket household a kitten free zone.

There was no evidence of the previous day's exertions on Leontiade's features as he snoozed in a comfortable armchair in the kitchen. The kitchen was delightfully cool, in contrast to the heat outside. It made me reflect that Marigold may have a point about installing air-conditioning; we were certainly finding it difficult to acclimatise to the July heat.

"I keep Leo busy today so he not be the trouble for Victor this evening," Sampaguita said when Spiros asked her how his uncle had been. "We took the short walk and Leo seemed quite lucid, he express the wish to go one day soon to the sea, he has the fond memories I think."

"Perhaps when the heat is not too the much for him," Spiros said. "Are you ready to go Sampaguita? I take you to the good restaurant on the coast with the fresh octopus. Perhaps later we can to stroll with the feet in the sea."

"That sounds lovely, Spiro. I have cooked the pork adobo dish for you Victor, I hope you enjoy this taste of my home. I must tell Leo we are leaving, it may unsettle him if he wakes to find Mr Bucket here and me gone."

Spiros gently shook Leontiades awake. The elderly gent immediately recognised his nephew, saying *"Spiro, agori mou."*

Fussing over his uncle, Spiros asked him if remembered me. The old man demonstrated his grasp on reality by recalling he'd met me in a garden and that I'd had a goat with me; even though the goat was nothing to do with me it was a pretty close proximation of our meeting for someone who was only with it half the time. Sampaguita told Leo that I'd brought him a gift of a kitten, tenderly relinquishing Tesco onto his lap where the pair immediately bonded, the kitten attaching its tiny claws to Leo's pyjama legs, purring contentedly as Leo stroked it.

"Victor, Leo will tire very soon, please to help him to the bedroom and bring to him the nightcap," Sampaguita said.

"A nice mug of cocoa, perhaps?" I suggested.

"The uncle sleep the better with the glass of Metaxa," Spiros clarified, ushering Sampaguita out to the hearse.

I decided to delay sampling the pork adobo until Leontiades retired for the night. Since he seemed content to sit quietly stroking the kitten and not engage in conversation I spread my books out on the kitchen table, needing to swat up on Greek speciality foods before guiding a group of holidaymakers on the Greek gastronomic tour. With the first tour scheduled to take place *methavrio* I had less than thirty-six hours to hone my knowledge of the subject.

It struck me that talking about the various foods which the ancient Greeks considered to have aphrodisiacal qualities would make an excellent introduction to my tour. Poring over my books I scribbled notes that I could later fashion into a speech. I would begin by explaining that the word aphrodisiac is derived from Aphrodite, the Greek goddess of love and beauty. In art form she is often depicted emerging from the ocean in a seashell, hence the belief that oysters and clams have aphrodisiacal qualities. I hoped that some of the excellent fish stalls in the market would have an abundance of oysters and clams I could point to whilst reciting my speech, though it may be prudent to advise the group not to purchase any in case they turned in the heat. Some of the specialist shopkeepers may not be too welcoming if my little excursion attracted a posse of stray cats desperate to get their paws on bags of shellfish.

I was actually surprised to read that the ancients regarded garlic as an aphrodisiac, considering the rather primitive mix of powdered ashes, oyster shells and crushed bones that passed as tooth-powder back in the day was somewhat lacking in minty freshness. Although I am certainly partial to the addition of fresh garlic in my cooking, I find the notion of eating the stuff raw rather repugnant. I wondered if Litsa's brother, who famously adds raw garlic to his taverna bread, uses it as a crude Viagra substitute. I decided to mention his garlic habit on my tour, the local detail would be sure to serve as an amusing anecdote.

I read with interest that saffron harvested from the crocus flowers of Krokohoria, the crocus villages of Kozani, has also been considered an aphrodisiac since ancient times. I would weave into my spiel the story of Hermes and Krokos, explaining how legend has it that the purple flowers that carpet Kozani originally bloomed from a drop of Krokos' blood. I was sure one of the shops in the old quarter would carry a supply of *krokos* for my charges to snap up if they were inspired by its history.

"*O Spiro, ferei Metaxa.*" Leontiades' words broke my concentration; looking at my watch I was surprised to discover I'd been engrossed in my books for almost an hour until the old fellow disturbed me by asking for his nightcap. It was time to give Leontiades a hand to bed and tuck him up with a glass of Metaxa. I noticed there was no sign of Tesco; it must have wandered off while Leo was dozing. I would search for the kitten once Leo was settled; if it had got out and headed back home I wasn't sure that I would be able to persuade Marigold to part with the wretched creature a second time.

As I helped Leo to his feet he had a lucid moment, realising I wasn't Spiros, "*den eisai Spiros.*"

Jogging his memory I said, "*Eimai Victor, thymasi,*" reminding him of my name. Peering at me through narrowed eyes, something deep in the recess of his mind clicked into place and he said "*i katsika.*" Assuming that he was associating me with the goat in Litsa's garden, rather than calling me an actual goat, I assisted him to the bedroom before going back to the kitchen to pour his drink. Returning with Spiros' brandy I tripped over something under foot and some of the five star liquid splashed out from the glass, soaking the top of Spiros' pyjamas.

"*Sygnomi, sygnomi,*" I cried, apologising as I mentally cursed Tesco for causing my clumsiness.

"*Den peirazei,*" it doesn't matter, Leo assured me as Tesco sprang onto his chest, snuggling close and lapping up the spilt brandy.

By the time I returned with some kitchen roll

to dab at Leo's soggy chest the old man was crooning an old Greek song to the sparked-out and possibly inebriated kitten. This picture of domestic contentment made me smile: I could honestly report to Marigold that Tesco had found a good and loving home.

Sampaguita's pork adobo was as delectably tender as Spiros had promised. It was my first time sampling Filipino food and I was impressed with the perfect balance of flavours. Tucking into the dish I reflected that it was rich in garlic. I chuckled at the thought that the ancient Greeks had not been correct about everything since the garlic was clearly having no discernible aphrodisiacal effect on me. After finishing my meal I washed the crockery, noting with approval that Sampaguita kept a gleamingly hygienic sink. I hoped that Spiros' efforts to work his charm were successful since it struck me that his fragrant Filipana flower would be an excellent match. My friend the undertaker was reaching the age where he should settle down and stop chasing tourist women.

Feeling the chill of the air conditioning I poured myself a glass of Metaxa and stepped outside. The evening was still warm, though no longer cloyingly humid. I had missed the sunset, but could still appreciate the stars in the night sky and the delicious scent from the lemon rosemary Sampaguita was cultivating in the garden. Sipping my brandy I relished the peace of the evening, realising there would be few opportunities for such peace once our visitors descended upon us on Sunday.

I was just considering a top-up when the beam of headlights heading up the narrow lane heralded the return of Spiros and his date. Although I assured Sampaguita that Leontiades was sleeping comfortably, she rushed inside to check on him, showing genuine concern. The lingering look she gave Spiros as she disappeared indoors made the question I asked Spiros superfluous.

"How did the evening go?"

"I bring the bottle and then to tell you," Spiros said, stepping into the kitchen for the bottle of Metaxa and another glass. After pouring us both a drink Spiros clutched his chest dramatically, saying, "Tonight was the *romantikos* and the Sampaguita feel it too. Our eyes make the love across the table, such the *romantikos*. And then we walk on the water and the kiss of the Sampaguita is like the butterfly wing on the lip."

"In the water, Spiro," I corrected.

"Maybe the other nights yes, but tonight I tell

you we walk on the water, Victor."

Chapter 20

Imported Spam

Although it wasn't late when I arrived home Barry and Cynthia had already retired for the night. I couldn't help but notice they shared a lot of early nights since they'd given up the virtuous pretence that Barry slept on the sofa. Marigold, waiting up for my return, informed me that Cynthia was apparently still stewing over her shredded veil but that she had proffered a reluctant apology of sorts for the way she had spoken to Marigold earlier. I agreed that my wife had not deserved the dressing down she'd received, but kept my suspicions to myself that Cynthia's own mutant cat had been the guilty party. A fleeting thought struck me before I dismissed it as absurd: perhaps Kouneli was cunning enough to have deliberately destroyed the veil in an effort to sabotage the wedding. Perhaps the vile mutant was jealous of Barry.

Marigold had attempted to make amends by hand washing the ruined bridal veil in gentle soapflakes, intending to take it along to the ladies' sewing circle the next morning to see if any of the Greek ladies could work their needlework magic on the bedraggled rag.

Because Cynthia was working right up until the eve of her wedding so that she could take a few days off for the occasion, she had suggested to Marigold that I could perhaps drive up to town the next day to source a replacement veil. Knowing nothing at all about women's fashion I snorted at the very notion, seriously doubting if I would be able to tell the difference if Cynthia exchanged her vows with her head wrapped up in an old net curtain, a plastic bag, or an expensive veil.

With my repping schedule I had little enough free time as it was and I had no intention of running about pandering to Cynthia's vanity. In my opinion it seemed a tad over the top to dress up in bridal wear at all since I had it on good authority that the mayor would make quick work of the marriage service at the *dimarcheio* and would be unlikely to even bother turning out in a tie to conduct the brief ceremony.

"I did tell her you'd be useless," Marigold assured me. "I said to her you can hardly expect a man who has no clue how completely styleless it is to pair socks with sandals, to go shopping for your wedding day."

"Well until someone concocts a mosquito repellent that can protect my ankles from the blood sucking biters, the socks are staying," I retorted. I was not unaware that Marigold considered my choice of clothing a tad staid, but she had long accepted it was not her place to dress me. The way Marigold occasionally shot a withering look at my habitual attire, anyone would think I wandered around in a sleeveless tank-top with a knotted hanky on my head, rather than a perfectly conventional outfit.

"I've been worrying about Tesco all evening," Marigold sighed.

"No need to worry, Leo and the kitten immediately formed a mutual admiration society, and Sampaguita was quite besotted with the creature," I said. "She did say you'd be most welcome to pop by and visit the kitten anytime."

"And how did you cope with babysitting Leo? Was it easier than dealing with Aunty Beryl?"

"He was no trouble at all. I managed to do quite a bit of reading up on speciality Greek foods in preparation for the gastronomic tour."

"That's nice dear," Marigold said disinterestedly. "What about Spiros' date, did it go well?"

"Exceptionally well I'd say, they were gazing at each other like a pair of love-struck teenagers when they returned. Spiros even confided they exchanged a kiss on the beach."

"Oh I'm delighted to hear it went off well, Sampaguita is just what Spiros needs and they do make a lovely couple. By the way Cynthia was saying that your boss, Tiffany is it, is thinking of adding a typical traditional Greek village taverna evening to the itinerary. She's added Meli to the shortlist of possible venues and will be popping into the taverna tomorrow evening to check it out," Marigold revealed. "Apparently she's got it into her head that it will be popular since she's heard it is so authentically Greek. She thinks that bread baked in the outside oven will serve as a big tourist draw."

"Good grief, that blasted Tiffany has gone too far. I refuse to have our local taverna overrun with coach trips of gawking tourists, it would ruin the ambiance," I said, horrified at the very suggestion.

"I have to say I agree with you..."

"Can you imagine the locals' reaction? It's the place they go to unwind at the end of the day, not be put on display as typically quaint Greek characters. I've never heard anything so ridiculous."

"Victor, I said I agree with you. Surely Nikos wouldn't go along with the idea, he's getting on a bit to cope with a coachload at his age," Marigold said.

"We must eat there tomorrow evening. When Tiffany turns up I can point out all the hygiene violations and convince her it is a terrible idea," I said, making a mental note to stop by the taverna the next morning and persuade Dina to attend the ladies' sewing circle rather than slopping the mop around the taverna. A good layer of dust should help to convince Tiffany the place was a filthy dump that tourists would never willingly frequent.

Before I had chance to compile a convincing list of drawbacks to put Tiffany off our local taverna, the telephone rang.

"Whoever can be calling at this late hour?" Marigold complained.

Being unfamiliar with the voice on the other end, I shrugged. The caller was a Greek woman speaking impeccable English, phoning on behalf of *Kapetanios* Vasos and a small group of French divers. She explained that the divers wished to privately charter Pegasus the following Tuesday, in order to chart the cold water springs in the sea. Since Vasos would be unable to communicate with the French party he needed me to go along and translate.

Although the under-the-table payment proposed was very tempting, I had to be honest and confess my French was limited to reciting the names of a few fancy Cordon Bleu dishes. The woman assured me that my lack of French would not be an issue since one of the divers had a smattering of English. Although I hated to turn the job down I explained to the caller that I was otherwise committed since my family were flying over on Sunday and I was planning some days out to show them the area. After conferring with the divers she assured me it would be no problem at all if I'd like to bring my family along for a free day trip on the boat. Needless to say I snapped her hand off, thinking my family would be delighted to join the excursion.

"That was a stroke of luck," I said to Marigold, relaying the call. We had been planning a couple of day trips to entertain our visitors in the run up the wedding. Although we both favoured visiting the Monastery of Elona with our house-guests, recommended to us by Lefteris, we had unfortunately ruled it out because we weren't sure how Violet Burke would cope with the one hundred step entrance.

"A day out on Pegasus does sound ideal, as long as Violet Burke isn't prone to seasickness," Marigold agreed, smiling in approval as Catastrophe sprang onto my lap and started licking my ear. The cat had made a remarkable recovery since losing part of its tail, its balance almost completely restored to normal. Reaching over to take my hand Marigold said, "I'm so happy to think in just three days Benjamin and Adam will be here, I do miss the boys."

The tender moment was interrupted by the telephone ringing again. Passing the cat to Marigold I answered the phone, mouthing to her, "It's Violet Burke." I still felt uncomfortable referring to the woman as my mother after she had so callously abandoned me in a bucket at the railway station as a baby.

BUCKET TO GREECE (VOL. 4)

With the receiver held at arm's length to spare my eardrums from being blasted, Marigold was able to listen in to the conversation. Even though Violet Burke would be travelling over with our son Benjamin and his life partner Adam, she wanted reassurance that I would indeed be collecting the threesome from the local airport and she wouldn't be forced to endure another long bus journey from Athens. The way she carried on anyone would think the bus trip from the capital was in some sort of peasant conveyance in a third world country, complete with barnyard livestock perched on the locals' laps.

Violet Burke expressed relief that I would indeed be collecting them at the local airport. She complained her suitcases were so heavy she could barely lift them up and wouldn't be able to cope with them on the bus. I assured her that as it was the height of summer she'd be able to travel light, needing only a few summer frocks and some swimwear. She then revealed she hadn't given a second thought to her wardrobe as yet since she'd been so busy stocking up on good British food she felt sure I must be missing.

"I remembered how much you liked your Fray and Bentos, and on top of that I got you half-a-dozen cans of Spam, some tinned mince, and some proper malt vinegar for your chips. I won't bother carting tins of mushy peas over; I'll throw some fresh ones from the chippie in a Tupperware dish before I leave," Violet Burke said.

"Tinned mince and Spam," Marigold mouthed at me, her face scrumpled in disgust. I had only managed to persuade her not to bin the stash of Fray and Bentos that Benjamin had brought over on his flying visit by convincing her we could feed them to my mother.

"There's really no need to bring all that food with you, the cupboards are already overflowing with Fray and Bentos. They'll charge you a small fortune at the airport for excess baggage weight," I reasoned.

"Well I don't know. Perhaps I'll just bring the Spam, it will save me forking out for a wedding present. I don't want to spend a lot because I can't say I took to that Cynthia."

"Hmmm," I said noncommittally, thinking it best not to mention she would have to share a bedroom with the bride-to-be.

"Now talking about the wedding, is there some sort of foreign dress code Victor?"

"There's no point in asking me about women's fashions, let me pass you to over to Marigold for a nice girly chat," I said, blithely ignoring the withering look my wife fired in my direction.

Chapter 21

Cut to the Quick

The electric pump feeding the back-up tank clanked and groaned in noisy complaint as I showered in barely a trickle of water. With the imminent arrival of our house guests the potential water shortage did not bode well, necessitating an implementation of strict rationing for the household. The cumulative groans of complaint upon receiving my instructions regarding domestic water rationing were loud enough to compete with the strange noises emanating from the pump, but I reassured everyone that I intended to have strict words with the authorities at the *dimarcheio,* to which I was heading that morning on another unrelated matter.

Ever since the aborted water protest I had been determined to become involved in local politics as a way of showing greater commitment to the community and demonstrating my natural leadership skills. Although never one to become embroiled with petty office politics at the council during my illustrious career as a public health inspector, I nevertheless felt I had plenty of political acumen to offer in my retirement.

I had compiled a list of suggestions to put to the local mayor regarding the serious matter of public bin hygiene, or rather the lack of it, which I intended to present to him that morning. It had been no easy matter translating the necessary phrases into Greek since I was unfamiliar with the technical terms for hygienic refuse disposal, spending many an hour sweating over the dictionary.

Whilst the public bins were a permanent eyesore marring the village, they were far more than a blot on the landscape in the summer heat. The fermenting stew of rotting rubbish encased in plastic bags unleashed a vile stench, reaching particularly noxious levels when the village strays foraged into bin territory, ripping the bags open with gay abandon in search of food, exposing a maggot ridden mass of pulsating discarded slop. To rub salt in the wound it was often days between collections.

When the garbage was finally taken away there was no effort made to sanitise the empty receptacles, thus the stench remained. Bags of rubbish tossed out of car windows often missed their target, and the refuse collectors were decidedly hit and miss in their approach to scooping it up, often not bothering. This lax attitude to cleaning the environment meant that plastic bags were often picked up on the breeze, landing in villagers' gardens, despoiling the countryside and presenting a choking risk to livestock.

Down on the coast the metal rubbish bins were supplemented with blue plastic ones for recycled waste, but we were afforded no such luxuries up in the village. Marigold had pointed out that no one paid any attention to the recycling labels plastered on the blue bins which ended up heaving with mixed household rubbish chucked in willy-nilly: I explained that was hardly the point, the village should be serviced with recycling bins and I would be happy to police them and educate the locals on their proper usage.

"I can't imagine why you think the mayor will listen to you, but if you want to waste your time..." Marigold said as the four of us finished our breakfast.

"I'm sure he will welcome my advice when I explain that I am a highly qualified *epitheoriti ygeias kai asfaleias* with many years of experience," I replied.

"An '*epitheo*' what?" Barry asked, spreading my homemade strawberry jam on the bread Dina had baked in her outside oven. My first foray into jam making had been an unqualified success.

"A health and safety inspector," I clarified.

"But you didn't have anything to do with public waste bins," Marigold pointed out. "I could understand why you think they might listen to you if you'd been a dustman."

Snorting into her coffee Cynthia scoffed, "You can't say dustman anymore, it's not politically correct, you have to call them waste management and disposal technicians."

I scowled at Cynthia. It had taken me ages to memorise my previous job title in Greek and I had no intention of leafing through my Greek dictionary to find the politically correct mouthful for dustman. Cynthia momentarily redeemed herself when she continued, "But Victor does have a point. We really ought to have recycling bins in the village. Barry and I will definitely be into recycling when we move into our new home."

"We wouldn't throw so much waste in the bins if Victor didn't object to us feeding leftover scraps to the chickens," Marigold complained.

"How many times do I need to explain that it is an insanitary practice that can spread disease? Unless you wish to run a vegan kitchen the chickens should not be fed on our leftovers," I scolded.

"You may have been an experienced health and safety inspector Victor, but I fail to see how that makes you an authority on what chickens should eat. People happily fed their livestock on scraps for years until busybodies like you started laying the law down and interfering with common practices," Cynthia opined in a mocking tone as she prepared to leave for work. "You came across as a pompous know-it-all when you were lecturing Nikos on the dangers of pig swill."

Barry studiously avoided my eye whilst Cynthia had her say. I was cut to the core, not so much by her thoughtless words, but by Barry's failure to leap to my defence like the good brother-in-law he is. Barry has always had my back until now and as an abandoned orphan I have always appreciated his brotherly support.

Cynthia left for work and the three of us finished our breakfast in silence, Marigold, her nose stuck in a Greek text book, oblivious to the atmosphere. Barry finally broke the awkward silence by reminding me that we were due to meet the notary at noon, along with Harold and the lawyer. With my plan to visit the mayor I had completely forgotten about the appointment. Still sulking over Barry's failure to curb his fiancés sharp tongue I reminded him that I had important business of my own to attend to at the *dimarcheio* and I was sure he wouldn't need me to hold his hand since Spiros would be there.

"Fine," Barry said, shuffling off with a hangdog expression, clearly cut to the quick by my dismissive attitude.

"Oh has Barry gone?" Marigold asked, realising the two of us were alone. "I don't know if I'll ever be able to get my head around so many different Greek tenses. I don't suppose the Greeks will mind if I just say everything in the present. I'd better get a move on. I have my Greek lesson and then the ladies' sewing circle. Now where did Cynthia leave that wretched veil?"

Marigold deposited a fond kiss on the top of my head as she headed off to the bedroom to get dressed, pausing to say, "Good luck with your bin thingy darling. I'm sure you'll make quite an impression on the mayor."

Chapter 22

Wracked with Guilt

I decided to walk over to the taverna to speak with Nikos before driving down to the *dimarcheio* to waylay the mayor. Just in case Tiffany turned up before me that evening I wanted to pre-empt her by filling Nikos in on her ludicrous idea to turn my local into a bustling tourist attraction. I only got as far as Kyria Maria's garden gate before I ran into Nikos exiting my neighbour's garden, dragging a familiar looking sheep by a rope. My hysterical neighbour, armed with a broom, was trying to shoo the animal out, shouting to Nikos, "*valte to provato sti souvla.*" Rolling his eyes Nikos told me that he had no intention of spit roasting the animal. He had a reputation for only cooking the finest lamb and the tough as old boots stubborn sheep was only fit for stuffing into a meat pie.

His point was moot since he was simply returning the persistent escapee to Panos' field. Nikos told me that Papas Andreas had telephoned him earlier to ask for his help in removing the sheep from his mother's garden because Panos was off somewhere on his tractor and the heathen sheep exhibited absolutely no respect for the clergyman's authority.

"Marigold and I had a run in with this sheep the other evening," I told Nikos.

"Yes, I hear you were the quaking with fear. It has the fearsome horns…"

"Nonsense, of course I wasn't frightened of the sheep, though it did unnerve Marigold. She's of a more delicate disposition than me."

Hastily changing the subject I explained to Nikos that my boss at the tour company had a ridiculous notion to turn his taverna into an authentic Greek attraction for coachloads of tourists and intended to turn up that evening to check the place out.

"If I want to be the attraction for the tourist I would to open my taverna on the coast where the foreign people throw the money," Nikos snorted. "If I want to be the rich I would to play the bou-zouki for the foreign tourist and not to toil in the fields. I have no the interest in cooking for for-eigns who take the tables from the locals. They expect a stupid menu with the choice of food, they want the rubbish shop bought wine and they demand the butter for the bread. This is not my way. The taverna is the simple place for gather-ing, to drink the *spitiko* with the friend, the place for the old people not to get lonely."

"I was hoping you'd look at it like that," I said. "I was horrified at the prospect of the ta-verna becoming overrun with tourists who would drive the locals out. It would probably help to put my boss off the idea completely if you don't bother cleaning today, just let the dust settle and make sure Dina doesn't throw any bleach in the toilet."

Fixing me with a piercing stare, Nikos strug-gled to keep a serious expression on his hand-some features. "You want the spit and sawdust look? You think I not to know that is what you foreigns say about the taverna?"

Unsure whether to stare Nikos down or admit

to his accusation, I was still dithering when he burst into laughter, saying "The spit and sawdust, you have the Greek humour Victor."

Relieved that he could see the funny side I was delighted when he added, "I give to you boss the flea in the ear. What you call him?"

"Tiffany, she's a jumped up twenty-something."

"Victor po-po, you have to answer to the girl, this must be the, how you say, emascapating for you," Nikos jeered.

"Emasculating," I corrected, "But actually my manhood is perfectly intact, thank you."

"Except when you to run into the fearsome sheep," Nikos laughed, managing to have the last word.

"We'll see you this evening Niko. I shall look forward to you putting Tiffany in her place."

"You can count on me. You want to drink coffee before I go to the field?"

"No thanks, I'm heading out to meet with the mayor," I said, hopeful I would be able to impress all the locals that evening by telling them the mayor insisted I take charge of all local sanitary arrangements pertaining to the public bins.

The doors to various offices were open as I walked

through the corridors of the dimarcheio, local council workers looking up with disinterest at the sound of my footsteps. Having no clue which office I should enter to ask to meet with the mayor, I selected one at random, coughing politely to attract the attention of the woman who didn't bother to look up from her screen. As I started to speak she held up a finger to indicate I should wait before she resumed her painfully slow two-fingered typing. When she finally deigned to look up I cleared my throat before reciting the sentence I had carefully rehearsed in Greek: I would like to meet with the mayor.

"Tha ithela na synantitho me ton dimarcheio."

"Den einai etho, einai se kideia," she responded, telling me he was not there, he was attending a funeral.

On the off-chance that the mayor might not be available I had prepared a second carefully rehearsed sentence, asking to meet with the deputy mayor. The disinterested employee sighed in annoyance as I slowly made my second request.

"Tha ithela na synanthitho me ton antidimarcho."

"Den einai etho, einai se kideai," she replied, telling me he was not there, he was attending a funeral.

I was rather taken aback by this response, unprepared for both of the local dignitaries to be off gadding at a funeral at the same time. It was most inconvenient, putting a spanner in my pre-translated spiel.

"*Kapoios allos simantikos edo*?" I said, asking if there was anyone else there of importance.

Raising an eyebrow in amusement the woman called out to the man in the office across the corridor, "*Luka, eiste simantikoi*?" asking him if he was important.

"*Ochi.*" Lukas shouted no.

"*Pes mou, ti theleis*?" The previously disinterested woman decided to take pity on me, saying tell me, what do you want.

Referring to the paper on which I had scribbled some pertinent Greek words I said, "*Thelo na miliso yia tous vromikous kadous*," advising her I wished to speak about the dirty bins.

Looking at me rather blankly she asked, "*Milas Ellinika*?"

I was unsure how to respond to the question 'do you speak Greek?' considering I had been speaking the language for the last ten minutes. I could feel my face flushing when the woman relented, saying "tell to me in English what you want."

"I would like to meet with someone to discuss

the filthy state of the public bins in Meli. I have some important proposals regarding implementing a recycling and sanitising regimen," I said.

"*Den katalavaino*," the woman said, telling me she didn't understand. "Come back on the other day."

"*Alla…*" I began to say 'but' before realising I was getting nowhere. A sudden thought occurred to me. I would telephone my good friend Spiros and ask him to explain the purpose of my visit to the woman.

"*O filos mou Spiros einai ena tilefono*," I said pulling out my mobile. Her rather bemused look made me realise that by this point my Greek grammar had gone completely out of the window and instead of saying I would telephone my friend Spiros I had actually said my friend Spiros is a telephone.

Moving into the corridor for privacy I dialled Spiros' number.

"Victor, I cannot to talk now, I do the funeral," Spiros said before terminating the call abruptly.

It occurred to me that there must have been a sudden death locally as Spiros hadn't mentioned the previous evening that he was doing a funeral today. It also occurred to me that both the mayor and the deputy-mayor were likely attending the funeral that Spiros was in charge of. A sudden third thought struck me: if Spiros was tied up with funeral arrangements he would have been forced to cancel attending the important notary's meeting pertaining to Barry's house purchase. Barry could be facing the meeting alone with no moral support, at a loss, out of his depth, confused by the unfamiliar Greek proceedings.

"Prepei na fygo, echo ena emergency," I called out to the woman I'd been dealing with, explaining I must go as I legged it at speed back to the Punto.

As I ran to the car waves of shame washed over me and I could feel the painful stab of remorse. How could I have abandoned Barry and let him down, Barry who had always had my back, who looked up to me as an elder brother and always valued my wise advice?

I had allowed my judgement to be clouded by my irritation towards Cynthia, never considering that Barry was no more responsible for the vicious words that came out of her mouth than I was for some of the thoughtless things that Marigold blurted out. Instead of expecting Barry to have leapt to my defence that morning I should have realised that he'd felt obliged to bite his tongue in order to keep the peace with the woman who was soon to become his wife. No matter how frustrating Marigold could be, I would always stand by her. Barry was surely only following my chivalrous example by putting Cynthia's feelings first.

Sprinting through the narrow streets, I garnered a few curious glances, the Greeks unaccustomed to the sight of a smartly dressed English man running in such an ungainly manner. I reflected that I would likely have attracted just as many peculiar stares if I'd been kitted out in luminous exercise gear, since joggers who run in the mid-day heat were generally regarded as foreign oddities.

Dripping with sweat, I arrived at the Punto and checked the time. The meeting was taking place in the small fishing village where I'd so nearly flopped from the diving board. I calculated that with almost half-an-hour to spare before the noon appointment with the notary I could make it if I put my foot down and could find a parking space. With my hand on the horn I recklessly overtook a dawdling camper van with Italian number plates, a donkey, and a defiantly helmetless Papas riding a moped, before reaching the village where I risked a huge parking fine by illegally parking the Punto next to a No Parking sign in front of the church. Never one to flaunt the rules lightly, I felt a stab of guilt. Choosing to ignore it I hot-footed it to the meeting venue, almost colliding with Barry in the entranceway.

His face creased in delight, Barry smothered me in a brotherly hug, exclaiming "Victor, you came. I knew you wouldn't let me down."

"Never Barry. Forgive me for being such an obstinate dunderhead this morning."

"There's nothing to forgive, I should have put Cynthia in her place; she had no business speaking to you like that."

"You aren't responsible for what comes out of her mouth."

"Oy, get a room you two." The moment of brotherly reconciliation was rudely interrupted by Harold's ignorant comment. "Fancy a bevy now that's out of the way?"

"What does he mean, out of the way? It's only just noon?" I asked Barry.

"The lawyer phoned to bring the appointment forward. There's no need to look so distraught Victor, Vangelis came along with me to make sure I understood all the nuts and bolts of what was going on."

"He's certainly a gem," I said in relief, pleased

that the builder had been there to support Barry. "So is all the paperwork sorted to go ahead?"

"Every last I dotted and every T crossed," Barry confirmed. "We get the keys on the morning of the wedding. It's all arranged that I'll send Harold an electronic transfer for the balance via the lawyer as soon as the keys are handed over. Ah, here's Vangelis now."

"*Yassou* Victor, I come with the Barry because the Spiros have the funeral to do."

"Yes, the funeral is quite the draw, the mayor and his deputy are both attending."

Barry and Vangelis looked at me quizzically, wondering how I was such a mine of information. "It's a long story," I said, suddenly remembering I had left the Punto parked illegally. It would be just my luck to discover the police had removed the number plates, prepared to hold them hostage until the fine was paid.

"So about that drink," Harold said.

"I must move the car," I said.

"And we have to get back to work, we've a big job on in Nektar," Barry said. "Anyway Harold, I don't think you've got time to sit around drinking, you've got some packing to do. It could get expensive if you aren't out of the place by next Thursday. Just think of those penalty clauses that the lawyer inserted into the contract."

"I can't be doing with nit-picking types like that. I suppose I'd best come back up to the village with you Barry, Joan will have my guts for garters if I don't help her with the endless packing. Pop round for a drink before we make the off Vic," he invited.

"All the best back in old Blighty," I replied, offering a handshake. Harold just nodded resignedly, knowing full well I would never take him up on his invitation.

Chapter 23

Better Preserved than Victor

Greatly relieved to discover that my bout of illegal parking had gone unnoticed by the powers that be I vowed never to take such a risk again. Recklessly flouting the law is one typical Greek trait I have no desire to emulate. I never fail to cringe and imagine imminent arrest when I am out and about with Spiros and he thoughtlessly parks the hearse on a pavement, or lights up a cigarette under a No Smoking sign.

I drove home to an empty house. Barry and Cynthia were both at work, and Marigold had no doubt gone straight from her Greek class to the ladies' sewing circle. I reflected that following the difficulties I'd had communicating at the *dimarcheio* it might be a good move to resume formal Greek lessons and join Marigold in future classes.

Hot and sweaty from my earlier exertions I was delighted to discover that the water supply was back to full pressure, the pump blissfully silent. Stripping off my sweat sodden clothes, still damp from my earlier exertions, I luxuriated in a long shower before contemplating lunch. Deciding to toss together a salad from fresh ingredients growing in the garden I stepped outside, thinking that if Kyria Maria was outdoors I would practice my Greek on her. Alas there was no sign of the elderly woman so instead I engaged in a one-sided conversation with the disinterested chickens. Their lack of engagement plus their studied pecking reminded me of the woman in the *dimarcheio* and the way she had ignored me whilst tapping away at her keyboard.

Recently Marigold had been dropping hints about putting Raki in the cooking pot, but having grown quite fond of my brood I could not in all conscience condone chicken murder, especially if it involved getting feathers on my hands. I reflected that if my wife continued to harbour such callous thoughts I may have to plead vegetarianism, though how convincing a pretence I could maintain when exposed to the temptations of Nikos' grill, was doubtful.

Surveying the garden I admired the budding evidence of the fruit of my labours, feeling a sense of accomplishment. Naturally I assigned some credit to Guzim for his help in transforming the overgrown weed infested wilderness into neat order. Marigold also deserves a mention for cultivating such a charming herb garden.

Selecting the most perfectly ripe tomatoes on the vine I added a gleaming green pepper to my lunchtime bounty and some fragrantly fresh basil leaves. The cucumber I picked was so weirdly curved that it defiantly flouted the 'practically straight' EU regulations, but I felt no compunction in defying such piddling bureaucracy.

Back in the kitchen I added a *feta* of feta to the salad bowl, as always amused that the Greek word for slice is the same word as the name of the national cheese. I threw in a handful of Dina's home preserved olives before dousing the salad in a liberal quantity of extra virgin olive oil. After topping up the cats' water bowls I carried the salad out to the balcony, appreciating the ambrosial flavours whilst basking in the beautiful view, the melodic strain of my favourite opera playing softly in the background.

With my appetite sated I decided to memorise some Greek phrases which may come in handy and help to hone my pronunciation. Marigold values her independence and may well complain I would cramp her style if I suddenly announced I would be joining her for Greek classes. After a tedious half-hour poring over my Greek phrase book I did some more research on Greek gastronomic delights in preparation for the next day's tour, before finally penning a couple of paragraphs of my moving abroad book.

It was late afternoon before Marigold returned, having enjoyed a long leisurely lunch at Athena's house in the company of the ladies from the sewing circle. My wife appeared in such good spirits that I didn't want to ruin the mood by voicing my reservations about the wisdom of eating food prepared in a kitchen that doubled up as a hair salon and was no doubt polluted by toxic hairsprays. Before I could enjoy a quiet moment alone with my wife to catch up with the news of our respective days, Cynthia returned home. I couldn't help bridling with annoyance, recalling her blatant rudeness over the breakfast table.

Cynthia immediately launched into what appeared to be a heartfelt apology for the critical words she had spewed earlier, begging my forgiveness for speaking so harshly. In the midst of her abject apology she told me that she had just run into Dimitris who had convinced her that I was actually an expert authority on swill, assuring her that indiscriminate livestock feeding can lead to the transfer of all manner of diseases.

"I should never have doubted or questioned your superior knowledge on the subject Victor," Cynthia grovelled. "I felt so foolish when Dimitris confirmed that swill should be avoided, I mean he is a learned professor so he must be right."

I didn't bother to enlighten Cynthia that the full total of Dimitris' knowledge about the dangers of feeding swill to his pig had come from me. There was no need for Cynthia to know that Dimitris was merely regurgitating the information I had given to him, or for her to realise it was actually pretty insulting that simply because he bore the epithet of professor she put more stock in Dimitris' knowledge than in mine.

"Victor, Marigold, I really do owe both of you apologies for the harsh way I have spoken to you recently. I had no right to be so sharp with you after you so kindly opened your home to me. All I can say is the stress of the wedding is getting to me, I had no idea how stressful it would become or that it would all get on top of me so much."

The tears streaming down Cynthia's face convinced me of her genuine remorse. I reflected that she had indeed had a lot to contend with recently; the sudden eviction from the rented house so soon after Barry moved in with her, the long hours she had been putting in at the tour company, the strain of living with her soon-to-be in-laws, and the stress of the upcoming wedding.

Despite their recent differences Marigold was clearly touched by Cynthia's tears, rushing forward to put a comforting arm around her. It was too much for Cynthia who broke into pitiful sobs, barely coherent as she spluttered, "I hate that I've turned into such a bridezilla, how could I have made such a fuss over that stupid veil? I've never been one to dream of a big white wedding, but every time I talk to my mother on the telephone she makes me feel inadequate because she is so critical about all the details, nagging me about not having a 'proper' gown or an aisle to walk down. All that money wasted on a pointless veil just to satisfy my mother's insistence that I ought to look virginal on my big day. Goodness knows what she'll say if she finds out that Barry hasn't really been sleeping on the sofa."

"I'm sure Barry will be happy to tell your mother he sleeps on the sofa..." Marigold suggested, handing Cynthia a large wad of kitchen roll to mop up the tears.

"Why should he, they are both grown-ups, not a pair of teenagers. This is the twenty-first century, not the Middle Ages," I interrupted. Even though I was yet to meet Cynthia's mother I had already taken a dislike to her due to her long distance interference over the reception. I reflected that it was probably best all round that Cynthia's parents were staying in a small hotel down on the coast during their visit as it would at least offer Cynthia some respite from her critical mother. I felt sorry for Barry, about to be stuck with a carping mother-in-law, particularly when I recalled his own late mother's practical approach to mine and Marigold's nuptials when it became clear a shot-gun wedding was necessary - and that had been back in the sixties when morality was much stricter.

"I'm dreading my parents arriving on Sunday. I worry they will disapprove of everything. They haven't even met Barry yet, but they can be so judgmental. Mother keeps warning me about marrying in haste and then having to lie in the bed I've made, but I love Barry," Cynthia gulped between sobs.

"Shush, don't get so upset," Marigold comforted. "I married Victor within five months of meeting him and I've never regretted our hasty decision in thirty-six years of marriage."

"And Barry is one in a million, any parents would be lucky to gain him as a son-in-law," I added. As I spoke I realised that Barry was made of strong stuff and if Cynthia's parents proved to be the in-laws from hell he would cope admirably: after all his sister had not signed up for Violet Burke, but she had made the best of the situation.

"You are both so kind, I don't deserve your understanding after being such a bridezilla," Cynthia cried.

"Of course you haven't been a bridezilla; it is only natural to get nervous before your wedding. Now go and wash those tears away before your face gets even blotchier," Marigold cooed.

As Cynthia disappeared to the bathroom Marigold sighed in relief. "Let's hope that really is the end of her bridezilla act, I don't know how much more of her histrionics I could tolerate."

"Did you mean it darling?" I asked.

"Of course, she's been completely over the

top. I don't know how Barry has put up with her since she turned into such a snivelling hysteric."

"I meant did you mean what you said about never once regretting marrying me."

Marigold looked at me intently, her eyes crinkling in a smile. "Ask me again in another thirty-six years."

The tender moment was interrupted by Barry's return. "Tell me the water's back and I don't have to ration my shower, I'm covered in sawdust from head to foot," he said in lieu of a more conventional greeting.

"Never mind the water, Cynthia's just had a bit of breakdown, pre-wedding nerves exacerbated by the prospect of her parents arriving," Marigold hissed.

"Oh no, has she gone and put her foot in it again?" Barry groaned, heading straight to the fridge for a Mythos, shedding sawdust all over the kitchen floor. "I'm going to have to say something to her, she was out of order this morning."

"No need, she's apologised, it's all water under the bridge now," I assured him.

"She's had a good cry to get it all out of her system," Marigold added to Barry's relief. "And when I show her what I've brought back from the ladies' sewing circle she's sure to cheer up. Go and find her Barry, she's in the bathroom, and tell her that I've got something very special for her."

"Barry, the water's back, you might want to shower first," I advised, grabbing the mop before Catastrophe could lick its way through any more of the sawdust.

When Cynthia and Barry re-joined us it was obvious that they had enjoyed a bit of making up, the only evidence of Cynthia's tears a couple of unsightly red bags below her eyes. I considered that Cynthia could distract attention away from the bags if she combed her glossy hair in a different style.

Clutching a Lidl carrier bag, Marigold said "Cynthia, I'm afraid that with all their combined needlework skills the ladies' of the sewing circle couldn't repair the damage that Tesco did to your veil." Delving into the bag she gently unfolded a beautiful piece of antique lace. "I brought this bridal veil home, if you like it you may wear it on your wedding day."

It appeared to my inexpert eyes that the veil was a delicate gossamer heirloom, embellished with the finest embroidery. Cynthia gasped aloud at the sight, barely daring to run the delicate fabric through her fingers.

"It's exquisite, the lace is so stunning. The embroidery is so captivating, look at the fine detail," she gushed. I considered that Cynthia really should come complete with an excess waterworks warning, her tears beginning to flow freely again. Marigold hastily moved the antique veil out of reach before it could suffer irreparable water damage.

"It belongs to Kyria Maria, she wore it for own wedding to Papas Andreas' father, who was also a Papas. The veil was a wedding gift to Maria, hand stitched by nuns from her father-in-law's parish."

"It's beautiful, and so carefully preserved," I observed. "Did Maria say what year she wore it?"

"She was just fifteen when she married in 1937."

I marvelled that although the veil was older than me, it was in much better condition.

"Of course it's just on loan, you'll need to return it to Kyria Maria after the wedding," Marigold said.

"I must go next door and thank her at once, it is such a generous gesture," Cynthia sobbed. "And to think I was so annoyed when she kept dropping hints about coming to the wedding. I can't believe I've been such a bridezilla."

Chapter 24

Sweet Chicken

Since Cynthia had promised to ditch the bridezilla obsession everything was back on an even keel in the Bucket household. A good few hours having passed without the bride-to-be dissolving into tears, I invited Barry and Cynthia to join us for the evening at the taverna. Cynthia wasn't overly keen on the idea of running into Tiffany on her evening off, but I promised her that Nikos and I had cooked up a plan that would put Tiffany's nose out of joint and bring her down a peg or two: possibly even enough pegs to lead to her demotion and Cynthia's promotion.

The four of us were just leaving the house when we were waylaid by an anxious looking Guzim asking if we had seen Doruntina. We greeted him with four blank stares until I recalled that Doruntina was the fancy name he gave to his pet rabbit. I asked Guzim when he had last seen the animal, remembering with dismay that Nikos had been planning to cook rabbit on the outdoor grill on the evening of Doreen's dinner party. To my great relief Guzim said that his floppy-eared bed fellow had been tucked up with him when he woke up that morning, but he hadn't seen her since he'd returned from work. It wouldn't do for Nikos to get a reputation for serving up the villagers' pets.

It really was a stroke of good luck that only that afternoon I had actually memorised an apt phrase which was tailor made for this situation. *"Tha kratiso ta matia mou xefloudismena,"* I said, lingering over my carefully enunciated pronunciation. Guzim stared at me mutely, an alarmed expression plastered on his face. Apparently the Albanian shed dweller was unfamiliar with the idiom 'I will keep my eyes peeled.'

"Yiati tha xekollisate ta matia sas?" he finally

asked in disbelief, wanting to know why I would peel my eyes, adding "*afto tha vlapsei.*" I supposed he had a point, if one literally peeled one's eyes it would indeed hurt. Assuring him we would look for the missing rabbit we continued on our way to the taverna.

"I'm sure there must be a perfectly innocent explanation but when I called in on Kyria Maria earlier there was a rabbit in her kitchen," Cynthia said.

"Alive or on the chopping block?" Barry queried.

"Oh, very much alive. Of course it may not have been Guzim's missing pet, but I didn't want to say anything to Guzim that might land Kyria Maria in it since it was so kind of her to lend me that beautiful bridal veil."

"For all we know she keeps rabbits, but it's best that you didn't say anything," I said. "The last time I saw Guzim's rabbit it was being pursued very aggressively by your cat."

Catching my eye and winking, Barry said "I'm sure you will miss Kouneli when we move out next week."

"I've just realised something odd," Marigold said. "In my Greek lesson this morning I learnt that the word *kouneli* is Greek for rabbit. Cynthia, did you confuse your cat with a bunny when you first took it in?"

Fortunately we arrived at the taverna before Tiffany put in an appearance. Whilst the others claimed an outside table Nikos and I huddled inside to finalise our plan. When Tiffany broached the question of using the taverna for organised tourist evenings Nikos would pretend not to understand a word of English. Since Tiffany's Greek was non-existent she would need to call upon me to translate. This would certainly demonstrate she was unsuitable to liaise with Greek businesses, being overly dependent on the underlings she likes to lord it over. It was a tad humiliating having to answer to a woman barely out of school uniform, but tonight I would turn the tables and leave Tiffany with egg on her face.

It struck me that whilst assiduously avoiding office politics back in England, I was taking an active interest here in Greece. Tiffany was all round too incompetent to hold a senior position. Hopefully word of her ineptitude in dealing with Greeks would get back to the higher-ups at the tour company, leading to her demotion and Cynthia's promotion. I felt no guilt at meddling. Tiffany would most likely land on her feet. It stuck me that she would be more suited to an organisational role in the company back in England where the locals were becoming immune to superfluous smatterings of 'like' infiltrating the language.

Since the primary objective this evening was to convince Tiffany that the taverna was a dirty dump not fit for tourists, I noted with approval the thick layer of dust carpeting the floor and the abundance of spider's webs hanging from the ceiling, clogged with mosquito corpses. Certainly if I was a self-respecting tourist with a modicum of care for basic restaurant hygiene I would flatly refuse to eat in such a clearly neglected and filthy establishment.

Taking my seat with the others I noticed that last night's breadcrumbs were still in evidence on the table. I smiled approvingly, recalling Tiffany was a stickler when it came to considering food a pollutant. I couldn't help but notice that the chairs were liberally decorated with black splodges from the night the ants went on their annual flight. If I hadn't been keen to make a bad impression on Tiffany I would definitely have words with Dina about her lackadaisical approach to cleaning since the presence of the splattered ants preceded that morning's conversation with Nikos about not slopping the mop about.

Dina slowly approached our table carrying olive oil and a basket of bread. She looked tired, Eleni by now too heavy with child to engage in anything more strenuous than idling in a chair and de-stringing green beans. Dina smothered me in one of her motherly embraces, whispering that it was very naughty of me to send the message that morning that she shouldn't bother cleaning that day. If the permanent spit and sawdust state of the surroundings didn't indicate otherwise anyone would have thought she was a veritable Mrs Mop.

When Nikos dumped a plastic bottle of *spitiko* wine on the table I suddenly recalled that I forgotten to pick Dimitris' brain about Greek wine in preparation for the gastronomic tour. If any of the tourists had questions about the subject I would come across as a woefully ill-prepared ignoramus. Realising I needed to urgently rectify the situation I implored Nikos, "I need you to tell me as much as you can about Greek wine."

"It is the simple Victor, if the *krassi* come from the shop it is rubbish, only the pure *spitiko* wine is free from the, how you say, preservatings and chemicals. You think the Dionysus, the god of wine, drink the shop bought muck?"

"I'm not disputing you make the best wine in

the world Niko..."

"And this year you promise to help to tread the grapes, remember?" Nikos reminded me, the Machiavellian smile curling his lip suggesting the taverna owner was scheming to take full advantage of my labour, rather than simply introduce me to a traditional custom.

"Yes of course, I'm looking forward to the authentic experience. But I have a dilemma Niko..."

"That's one of your words that translates the same," Barry piped up. "Did you know that the Greek word for dilemma is *dilemma*?"

Firing a look of exasperation at my brother-in-law I continued, "Look Niko, tomorrow I have to lead a guided tour around Greek speciality food shops and present myself as knowledgeable about Greek wines, but my dilemma is that I know nothing about them. I can't very well tell a group of interested tourists that all Greek wine that comes in a bottle is rubbish plonk, inferior to your homemade stuff. I'm sure they will rely on my recommendation to decide which wine to buy to take home."

"Why you not to say the wine is for the tourist, they can drink the shop bought rubbish, no problem, they not know the difference."

"Niko, help me out, tell me something interesting about Greek wine and add some historical context," I pleaded.

"The Greeks of course invent the wine and our ancient philosophers have the love for it, indeed it is considered the *afrodisiako*," Nikos said.

"Excellent, I've already prepared some spiel on aphrodisiacs."

"Now what to say of interest. Ah Victor, with your obsess about the hygiene you will like to know that the Hippocrates use the wine as the hygienic medicine to wash the wounds..."

"So they considered it had antiseptic qualities," I noted.

"Yes, it was the good disinfect," Nikos agreed.

"I suppose that must still apply to Retsina," Barry said. "It always reminds me of pine scented toilet cleaner, I can't stomach the stuff."

"That is because you only try the shop bought Barry, one day I make the *spitiko* Retsina and you taste the difference," Nikos said. "Many the ancients think the wine medicinal. The sweet wine was the good for the flatulence and the dark wine the good for the stunted growth," Nikos said.

"So which Greek wine should I recommend on the tour?"

"I think the Mavrodafni, it is the red and sweet," Nikos said before ambling over to the grill.

"There you go Victor, you know what to recommend to any flatulent tourists with stunted growth," Barry quipped.

"Mavrodafni would actually be an excellent wine to recommend Victor since it's a local wine, originating from the vineyards of the Peloponnese. It takes its name from the dark skinned grape it is made from which translates as black laurel," Cynthia said, surprising me with her expertise.

"I didn't know you were well up on Greek wine, that's most helpful, thank you," I said.

"I must confess to a certain weakness for Mavrodafni, I love its sweet potency and it marries wonderfully with figs and *manouri* cheese," Cynthia said.

"I wonder if it pairs well with chicken," Marigold said. "We have a chicken we called Mavrodafni, it would be quite amusing to roast it and then toast it with the wine it was named after."

"There will be no roasting of Mavrodafni on my watch," I said sternly.

"You'd prefer it in a curry?" Marigold asked.

"Mavrodafni is not for eating, she is an excellent layer and I refuse to be party to chicken murder," I insisted.

"But you don't object to eating plastic wrapped chickens from Lidl," Marigold pointed out.

"That is completely different. I haven't had the pleasure of getting to know a Lidl chicken on a personal basis before it meets an untimely end," I protested. "Over the weeks I have become quite familiar with the idiosyncrasies of each of my chickens. Did you know that Mythos likes to follow me around and loves to be petted?"

"You can't go getting attached to the livestock Victor," Cynthia said.

"Oh I don't know, I think it's rather sweet that Victor is growing attached to the chickens, as long as he doesn't expect me to give them house room. Perhaps there's still hope that he will develop affection for the remaining kitten," Marigold said, her voice dripping in sarcasm.

Chapter 25

A Nasty Case of Leather Jacket

Whilst we tucked into salad and cheese Nikos threw some lamb chops on the grill. Basking in the delightful breeze we were grateful that we had made the choice to live in a mountain village rather than down on the hot and humid coast. Watching lights sporadically drift across the dark sea in the distance we speculated if the fishermen were in for a good catch, Marigold suggesting that we drive down to the local harbour the next morning to snap up some freshly caught fish. Smiling fondly at my wife I knew full well she would never be able to drag herself out of bed in time to take advantage of the early morning catch, but rather than point out the obvious I simply reminded her that I would be in town the next day leading the gastronomic tour.

I watched with interest as Nikos greeted the locals with his typical enthusiasm. I noticed they all selected outside tables close to the smoky grill, shunning the tables inside the overheated taverna with its fluorescent lights, apparently happy to eat outdoors now that the annual flight of flying ants was safely out of the way for another year. The strong smell of vinegar preceded Litsa's brother when he wandered over to exchange pleasantries, clearly another fan of Barry's preferred method of keeping the mosquitoes at bay. Obviously the vinegar was effective as the nearest mosquito ignored Litsa's brother, instead honing in on my bare shins. Marigold sent me a sympathetic look when I suddenly winced in pain, suffering another bite. Rummaging through her handbag she passed me a jar of Marmite to rub into my exposed bits.

Plucking the jar from my hand with interest Litsa' brother asked what it was, "*Ti einai afto*?" To my shame I realised I had no idea of his actual name. It struck me that if I suddenly asked him his name it would look odd, if not downright rude, that I was clueless after almost a year of acquaintance.

"*Einai Marmatis, thes na dokimaseis Kyrios Kosta*?" Cynthia said, inviting the old fellow, who it turned out was named Kostas, to try the Marmite.

Cynthia spread a generous amount of my mosquito repellent on a piece of bread for Kostas to sample. Staring suspiciously at the sticky brown paste he took a reluctant bite, rolling it around his mouth and chewing it slowly, mulling the flavours with a look of ambivalence on his face. We waited with bated breath for Kostas to either spit it out in disgust or to share his opinion of this novel foreign foodstuff, amused when he decisively proclaimed "*tha itan pio nostimo me to skordo*": it would be tastier with garlic. Personally I considered that a topping of raw garlic would only make the salty paste taste even more repugnant. Before I could reclaim the jar and smear some of its contents on my vulnerable shins Kostas had wandered away with it, eager to show it to his cronies.

"Take the vinegar," Barry invited, chortling when I finally gave in and rubbed some into my exposed bits. Better to smell like a chip shop rather than be a magnet for mossies.

"They laugh at you Victor, that you eat the stuff in the jar," Nikos said, placing a large platter of juicy lamb chops on our table and nodding towards the table of bemused looking elderly local men sampling the Marmite.

"The laugh is on them Niko, I wouldn't dream of eating the horrid stuff, I simply rub it in to keep the mosquitoes away."

The laughter drifting across from their table came to an abrupt end when Nikos shouted over, telling them they were the fools because rather than being edible the Marmite was actually a British mosquito deterrent.

"There's Panos," Barry pointed out as the welly clad farmer put in an appearance, waving across genially as he joined the table of elderly gents. I made a mental note to grab a quiet moment alone with him later to have words about his stubborn sheep.

"And there's Tiffany," Cynthia hissed. Our boss hovered tentatively just beyond the taverna's seating area, seemingly nervous and unsure whether to approach Nikos at the grill.

"I suppose I'd better make my presence known," I said, reluctantly leaving my companions to stake first claim on the lamb chops.

"Rather you than me, I'm in no mood to put up with her condescending ways," Cynthia muttered.

Tiffany stuck out like a sore thumb in our humble local taverna, attracting suspicious stares, standing out like a glowing beacon in her overly-tight orange repping uniform. As I approached her it was clear that she was relieved to see me.

"Still sporting orange I see Tiffany," I wryly observed.

"The new uniform like brought me out in a really nasty like itchy rash. I had to go to the doctor and he said I'd got some like horrible condition called *dermatino boufan*. I don't really understand what it is because he said it in like Greek, but he did prescribe some cream," Tiffany said as I tried to avoid staring at the angry red rash erupting from her cleavage.

"You really should take someone along with you who can get by in the language if you need to visit medical professionals Tiffany. I rather suppose that the doctor actually diagnosed you with the common condition of contact dermatitis, rather than the lesser known ailment of horrible leather jacket," I said, struggling to keep a straight face.

"I don't, like, understand you," Tiffany said.

"Well you just told me that the doctor said you had a horrible case of *dermatino boufan* which means leather jacket in Greek. Of course he may have been casting aspersions on your choice of clothing, but I think a diagnosis of contact dermatitis is far more likely. Some people are prone to suffer an allergic reaction to manmade fibres such as orange polyester or the cheap modacrylic which the new uniforms are fashioned from."

"We wouldn't have had to like change to new uniforms if some busy body hadn't kept stuffing like complaints about the orange uniforms into the suggestion box," Tiffany complained, clearly clueless I was the elusive suggestion box stuffing culprit.

"Not everyone can carry off orange as well as you Tiffany," I said, realising she was far too thick to spot my sarcasm.

"Oh, like thanks."

"Now I believe you've come up to Meli to consider the taverna as a tourist venue for an authentic Greek evening, a wise choice indeed, you won't find anything more authentic than this place. Let me show you inside," I invited, eager to see her reaction. "Do be careful not to lean against anything, I'm not sure that nasty infestation of cockroaches is under control just yet. Still they're sure to appeal to any of the usual little Johnnies on the trip, mischievous boys do tend to find cockroaches quite fascinating and any little Johnnies will be sure to smuggle a few back onto the coach."

The look of sheer horror on Tiffany's face was starkly illuminated in the hideous glow of the fluorescent lights, casting their beam on the thick layer of dust carpeting the floor and drawing attention to the mosquito clogged cobwebs. I'd had a whispered word with Dina earlier, persuading her to wipe the usual warm smile off her face and glower at Tiffany when she turned up. Dina was like putty in my hands, willing to do anything to oblige me, having grown very fond of me after I'd come to the rescue by standing in for her in the kitchen when she'd broken her arm. I was surprised by how much Dina excelled in the role, suppressing her usually friendly smile and adopting a scowling countenance. She deserved an Oscar for her performance, adding a lovely touch by sharpening a meat cleaver in a decidedly menacing manner while looking daggers at the interloper.

"It's not like what I expected, it's a bit... like,

dirty," Tiffany hissed, peering around nervously in case an imagined cockroach made a run through the dust.

"It's okay, you can speak up, no one here speaks a word of English," I assured her. "In fact the locals in general aren't at all friendly; they can be positively hostile to foreigners."

"I can see that. The old woman looks like really scary," Tiffany gulped. I had to bite my lip to prevent myself from bursting into laughter: the very idea of sweet lovely Dina who would do anything for anyone being actually scary was the most ludicrous thing I'd ever heard.

"She's in charge of the kitchen and her husband mans the grill," I said.

"Is the kitchen like as filthy as the rest of the place?" Tiffany asked, visibly shuddering and making no effort to hide her expression of bewildered disgust. I imagined that the thought of a cockroach crawling out of the salad might be triggering for her.

"Well I don't know, I wouldn't fancy braving that meat cleaver the old woman is wielding, to find out," I said.

"Victor, I'm like really surprised you eat here, I thought you'd be, like fastidious, with having been like a public health inspector in England…"

"Well 'been' is the operative word there Tiffany. Once I retired I threw in my public health inspector hairnet, thus freeing myself from the constraints of petty bureaucracy and the piffling worries about the odd outbreak of E-coli. After all a bit of E-coli never killed anyone."

Tiffany gawped at me, her mouth hanging wide in disbelief.

"Actually," I continued "E-coli *can* be a killer, but it's more likely to bring on a nasty case of diarrhoea. Of course some of the larger tourists may welcome that as a great way to lose a few pounds, especially if they've been over indulging in Greek food during their holiday. Probably best not to mention it though when you try to sell tickets for the excursion; ignorance is probably best unless it can be proved that eating here actually triggered an E-Coli outbreak."

"But you, like eat here," Tiffany pointed out.

"Well I do eat here yes, but that doesn't mean I like it. Being stuck out here in the sticks doesn't leave us with much choice; it's the only taverna in the village. If we venture further afield I can't have a drink and drive home. At least in here I can down a glass of homemade wine. Nikos stomps the grapes with his own feet you know, though I rather suspect from the taste that he doesn't bother taking his socks off or washing his feet," I grimaced.

"It must be like horrible for you being stuck in this out of the way village with only like a filthy taverna and really like old unfriendly locals. Wouldn't it just be, like safer, for you to eat at home?" Tiffany said.

"Have you tasted my wife's cooking?" I demanded, hoping Marigold would forgive me for maligning her culinary prowess. "You may as well take a look outside now that you're here Tiffany. I hope you've sprayed yourself liberally with repellent, the place is a positive breeding ground for mosquitoes. I don't want you coming down with a nasty dose of West Nile fever."

"I never knew the Nile was like in Greece," Tiffany said in surprise. My mind boggled at the thought of Tiffany no doubt attempting to book an excursion to the Pyramids of Greece on her next day off.

All conversation came to an abrupt end as we stepped outside to be met with a hostile stare from Nikos and curious unsmiling fixed glances from the rest of the locals. Tiffany, being obviously as unfamiliar with the norms of village life as she was with the origins of mosquito borne viruses, had no idea that if she simply smiled at her audience and made an effort to greet them, their stern looks would dissolve into welcoming countenances.

"Is that old man like eating raw garlic off the blade of a knife?" Tiffany hissed.

"Yes indeed, it's a local tradition that everyone who eats here has to start their meal off with a bulb of raw garlic, it's an excellent way of lining the stomach against potential E-coli bugs and salmonella. I'm sure that the garlic will prove popular with the tourists since it's locally grown, unless they are too distracted by the cockroaches," I said, finding it hard to believe how gullible she was.

"Locally grown cockroaches?" Tiffany gasped.

"No garlic. The locals don't grow cockroaches, they breed them. For some reason they find it entertaining to gamble on cockroach races, unleashing them to scuttle across the tables. There isn't much else to do out in the sticks. Now let me introduce you to Nikos, I'm sure he'd be delighted to welcome a tourist excursion. It will be a great opportunity for him to inflate his already ridiculous prices. There's nothing he likes more than ripping off foreigners, I'm sure he charges me four times as much as he does the

Greeks," I blatantly lied. The only true word I had uttered was that Nikos' prices were ridiculous: ridiculously low.

Nikos snorted as I made the introductions. Staring Tiffany down in an intimidating manner he said *"afti i portokali friki einai to aftentiko sou."* Thinking Tiffany would not appreciate the way Nikos had just exclaimed 'this orange horror is your boss' I was about to mis-translate and say something innocuous when Tiffany got my hackles up, demanding in a strident tone "You'll have to translate."

"How on earth did you expect to manage once you arrived when you can't speak Greek? It was a stroke of luck I just happened to be here this evening Tiffany. If you haven't noticed it's actually like my night off and I really ought to like bill you for my translating services if you expect me to facilitate your plan to turn this grubby old place into a tourist attraction," I said.

Rolling his eyes Nikos put on a good show of appearing affronted when he snapped in Greek, "Grubby, it was you who told me not to clean."

"Just play along unless you want to be running round after coachloads of tourists," I fired back in what I suspect was very ungrammatical Greek.

"What is he saying?" Tiffany asked.

"Well Nikos is rather insulted that the tour company would send along someone who can't even speak Greek to conduct such important negotiations. He's a man of great importance you know. He says he will telephone the company tomorrow and demand to know why they sent a mere girl along to disrespect him."

Tiffany immediately reddened upon hearing my words, her face clashing hideously with the orange uniform.

"The company will never like agree to send coachloads of tourists here, it is too dirty," Tiffany said. "They have, like standards."

"I'll just tell the owner that you have other village tavernas to consider shall I, no point in riling him up when he's holding that dangerous looking skewer," I suggested.

"Right," she said, her weary tone reflecting her defeated air.

"And if I may make a suggestion, perhaps Cynthia should liaise with the other tavernas on your list since at least she has a basic grasp of the language."

"I thought they'd like make an effort to, learn like English, if they want to like attract British tourists," Tiffany said.

"Funny, I rather think they have same idea about the British learning Greek," I retorted. "Well I'd better get back to my lamb chops. It wouldn't do for my stomach to be rumbling on tomorrow's gastronomic tour."

Staring at me with a worried expression Tiffany suddenly produced a packet of digestive biscuits from her bag and pressed them on me. I felt a momentary twinge of guilt that whilst I was scheming to get her demoted she was capable of such a generous gesture, until she blew it by saying "If you like come down with E-coli before tomorrow's tour I'll have to like cover for you. It will be really like awkward for me because I don't know a thing about like Greek food or wine. Don't eat any of the food here, have these biscuits instead, it will be like safer. Less chance of you ringing in like sick tomorrow."

"That's very thoughtful of you, it would be terrible if you had to lead a tour you are clearly unprepared for," I said, waving her back to her car.

"I felt quite sorry for her," Marigold said as I rejoined the table.

"Don't waste your time, she speaks to us in the most condescending manner at work and is clearly unqualified for her position. She's just a glorified pen pusher with no people skills. And the way she runs after Sakis - everyone knows he's devoted to his girlfriend," Cynthia replied.

"Oh I didn't mean the way Victor made her look foolish, I'm sure she deserved it. I meant I felt sorry for her because she looked so dreadful in that ghastly orange uniform and she clearly hasn't got a clue how to do her hair," Marigold said. "She's never going to meet a nice young man for a summer romance if she goes around looking like that, maybe you should bring her over to Athena's kitchen to get her hair fixed..."

Marigold's words stopped abruptly mid-sentence, the colour draining from her face. "I don't believe it," she said, her finger quivering as she pointed across the taverna.

Tiffany hadn't quite made it to her car: instead she was frozen in place, hands held aloft as though she was being robbed at gun point. The fearsome horned stubborn sheep that had made such a nuisance of itself all week was standing firm between Tiffany and her vehicle, staring her down.

"You did the good Victor, the tourists keep away for sure. I not to like that girl, she stick her nose up. I try to think, the cousin has the something to do with the tour company," Nikos said, presenting me with a freshly cooked plate of lamb chops. "Eat, you need the meat, it must be the *emascupating* for you to have the stupid girl boss."

"Emasculating," I automatically corrected.

"There is nothing emasculated about Victor's manhood, but it must be infuriating to have to answer to an unqualified person," Marigold defended.

"It must be a bit of comedown for you after your illustrious career as a public health inspector," Cynthia said with no apparent trace of sarcasm. "If Tiffany does get demoted perhaps you should take the job, rather than me."

"Really I have no interest in taking on a full-time position now I've retired. Anyway I have far too much on with the chickens and the garden, and I expect once I get involved in local politics I won't have a moment to myself. I'm perfectly content to lead a couple of tours a week and stay out of office politics," I assured Cynthia.

"But you're so competent Victor," Cynthia said.

"It is you who deserves the promotion Cynthia, after all you have years' of experience in tourism. Victor just does it so that he doesn't vegetate in retirement," Marigold added.

"And it keeps him from getting under your feet," Barry joked.

Chapter 26

Walk, Talk and Taste

Apart from the small hiccup of temporarily losing a couple of my tourist charges, the Greek gastronomic tour was a resounding success. Twelve foodies in total signed up for the tour, sensibly arriving in flat shoes and sunhats as recommended. To my great relief no one had dragged along a little Johnny, the possibility of which I must confess I hadn't factored in when composing my spiel on aphrodisiacal foods, a subject not really suitable for young ears.

V.D. BUCKET

After explaining the excursion would combine walking, talking and tasting I began the tour with a guided walk through the local market, a veritable trove of locally grown fresh produce and freshly caught fish. As always the market bustled with activity, necessitating the continual blowing of my whistle in order to keep the group together, the odd straggler detouring from my chosen route to be swallowed up by the crowds, or lingering to stare in morbid fascination at a whole cockerel suspended by its feet, commenting you don't see many of those in Waitrose. They were clearly an upmarket bunch.

Gathering my charges together they delighted in sampling local cheeses, *kasseri, sfela, kefalotyri, mizithra,* and *manouri,* eagerly purchasing the ones they favoured. Taste testing *loukaniko portokali,* the local sausage flavoured with orange peel, was such a success that even the avowed vegetarian of the party was tempted to try it, throwing her principles to the wind. My prepared speech about shellfish as aphrodisiacs went down well in the fish market, received with a few ribald comments and winks.

The only awkward market moment occurred when Mrs Cook needed a toilet stop, but after sticking her head round the door of the market loos and discovering they were of the primitive hole in the floor variety she pronounced that she would keep her legs crossed until we reached the historical quarter of town. Strolling through the historic streets to reach the family owned speciality food shops where more opportunities to taste Greek gastronomic delights awaited us, the group kept up a steady stream of questions, fascinated to learn more about traditional local foods.

The group sampled *horiatiko psomi*, local country bread, and *xera syka*, dried figs, in the speciality bakery, and sniffed the aromatic *kokkoi kafe*, coffee beans, in the traditional shop selling coffee, herbs and local olive oil. I think it is fair to say that the highlight of the tasting tour was the sampling of local Mani honey, truly the food of the gods. I explained that the ancients appreciated the beneficial and medicinal qualities of *meli*. The group were intrigued to hear that Spartan youths ate an exclusive diet of *meli* during their month of military training on Mount Taygetus. Perhaps inspired by my words the tourists snapped up jars of aromatic wild flower, thyme, and orange blossom *meli* to take back to England.

Whilst the group browsed the shops I purchased some pistachio *halva*, a traditional Greek sweet made from tahini, as a treat for Marigold. For some inexplicable reason my wife loves the stuff, but I fail to see the attraction as it gets stuck in my teeth. With the retail therapy behind us the group staggered under the weight of their bulging bags, finishing the tour with a traditional Greek lunch. I was delighted to note glowing reviews on the customer satisfaction surveys completed over lunch, everyone assuring me the tour had been most fascinating and enjoyable, promising they would recommend it highly.

Returning to the office after the tour I wasn't sure what to expect. Nikos had phoned me earlier to say that after much head scratching he had worked out his nepotistic connection to the tour company: his cousin's daughter's husband coincidentally happening to be one of the higher ups on the ground in Greece. Nikos had placed a call to his distant relative, complaining that he had found it very insulting that the company had sent a slip of a girl who couldn't speak Greek to negotiate the use of his taverna for tourist excursions. His cousin's daughter's husband had taken his complaint seriously, apologising to Nikos for the lack of professionalism and assuring him that in future they would use more mature representatives with at least a basic grasp of the language.

I felt a twinge of guilt when Nikos pronounced Tiffany was surely facing the chop. In light of his call what I didn't expect was an announcement shortly after my return to the office that Tiffany had been promoted.

"How did the first gastronomic tour go, was it like a success?" Tiffany asked.

"A resounding success indeed."

"So you didn't lose like any tourists then?"

"Only temporarily, all present and accounted for at the end of the excursion."

"I was up half the night worrying that you'd like come down with E-Coli from eating in that like filthy taverna, and I'd have to like lead the tour for you," Tiffany complained.

"It is advisable to be prepared for all eventualities Tiffany. When you are in charge you must be ready to step into the breach," I advised.

My smugness was not misplaced; if anything happened to prevent Cynthia leading a tour to Vathia or the Caves of Diros I was well prepared to take her place. Even though I had never been on either of the organised trips I had done extensive research in case I was needed to provide emergency cover.

"Well I think it's like too stressful. I'm happier

in the office than like having to deal with tourists," Tiffany said, skimming the comments on the customer satisfaction surveys. "Gosh, you've got like really high scores. I'm like surprised the company hasn't promoted you instead of like Cynthia."

"Cynthia's been promoted?" I said.

"You may as well like know. I've been given a new job, like a really big promotion, so Cynthia is being like promoted into my job here."

"You've been promoted," I exclaimed in surprise.

"I'm being like sent back to England to work in the office. It is like a really important job. I will be in charge of telling new reps about the importance of not like losing tourists and the importance of making sure all the customer satisfaction surveys are like completed."

"Gosh, that does sound like important," I said, imagining Tiffany would be in her element going full on jobsworth, lording it over some wet behind the ears new recruits. "So you're pleased at the prospect of returning to England?"

"I am, they don't like let sheep into the restaurants there. Living in Greece is like too worrying. Ever since seeing how like filthy that taverna was last night I've been imagining like picking up another disease."

"Another disease?" I queried, stepping back in case she was contagious.

"Like that rash," she clarified.

"Ah yes, the perplexing case of horrible leather jacket."

Peering at me through narrowed eyes Tiffany's mouth opened and closed soundlessly, reminding me of a startled goldfish. Detecting sarcasm was clearly too taxing for her brain.

"The job in like England won't involve dealing with the public."

"No more putting up with little Johnnies or their nightmare parents," I said.

"And everyone will like speak English."

"English like yours." My sarcastic quip went way over her head.

"I have to stay in Greece until like Cynthia comes back to work after her like wedding, then she'll do like my job here and I can go back to England."

"Well congratulations on your promotion Tiffany," I said sincerely, even though I suspected she'd actually been demoted.

Chapter 27

Toasting the Future

Driving home I reflected that the walk, talk and taste excursion had been most enjoyable. I would certainly be happy to lead more gastronomic tours throughout the season and establish my expert credentials as a foodie aficionado. Since the tour had ended after lunch the rest of my day was free and I decided to try and persuade Marigold to join me for a dip at the coast. I had some good news to share with my wife that was sure to put a smile on her face: Panos' stubborn sheep would no longer be stalking the village streets, staring down nervous types with its demonic eyes.

Passing through the village that morning I had come across Panos loading said sheep into his tractor. If I understood his Greek correctly he was transporting the sheep to pastures new because it was feeling out of sorts. Although Panos' explanation was a tad challenging for my Greek comprehension he helped me to understand by interspersing his speech with myriad gesticulations. Apparently the sheep had suffered the misfortune of losing its libido and with no urge to rut it had refused to stay with the rest of the flock, hence its constant straying. Panos had found the sheep a new home where it would no longer be required to perform during the mating season, making it sound like a cosy billet for retired ovines. I hoped he wasn't pulling the wool over my eyes by secretly sending the stubborn creature off to the abattoir.

Passing the look-out point on the mountain drive home I noticed a couple of members of the fire-brigade keeping watch for the first sign of summer fires. Stopping briefly I praised their sterling efforts, offering them bottles of chilled water from my cooler box which they graciously accepted. I was about to tell them about my crazy neighbour's former habit of burning plastic in her garden every morning, but decided that since I had only mastered the present tense it may not be a wise topic to introduce. I would feel terrible if my imprecise Greek led to a misunderstanding and Kyria Maria was carted away as a budding arsonist.

Arriving home I cast an approving look over the garden and exchanged pleasantries with the chickens, relieved that Marigold was no longer gunning to add any of them to the pot. Noticing that Guzim's rabbit was inside the coop with the chickens I was grateful that the Albanian shed dweller's beloved pet had returned to the fold. Guzim would have been inconsolable if the creature had pulled a permanent disappearing act.

Stepping into the house I entered a scene of utter chaos, almost falling over Kyria Maria who was furiously attacking a mattress propped up by the front door with a carpet beater. Marigold was practically buried beneath the weight of the spare room mattress she was dragging outside. Every piece of furniture had been moved, bedding lay discarded on the floor, and the contents of the kitchen cupboards spilled over every surface as though waiting to be polished and alphabetically rearranged. It appeared that my wife was engaging in an obsessive bout of spring cleaning, even though it was July. I had no idea how she'd managed to rope in the old woman from next door to get in on the act.

"Oh give me a hand Victor, I must get this mattress aired before your mother arrives, it has a definite whiff of vinegar about it. You can help me clean out your office for the boys, and make up the sofa for Barry. I shouldn't have left everything to the last minute, luckily Kyria Maria volunteered to lend a hand," Marigold cried. "I can just imagine Violet Burke's face if everything isn't in pristine order. She's worse than you for being fussy about having everything spotless. I just know that she will sniff out any dead mosquitoes that I neglect to sweep out from under the bed."

"Is all this really necessary, it's not as if the house wasn't clean to start with? Surely a little light dusting would have sufficed. There's no need to go overboard, we aren't picking them up from the airport until tomorrow afternoon."

"You'll have to go up to the airport without me Victor, there is still so much scrubbing to do..."

"But Benjamin will be expecting you," I said.

"It's not practical for us both go up, it will be too much of a squash to fit five us into the Punto,"

Marigold reasoned.

"Well someone can come back with Barry, there should be room in his van since he's only collecting Cynthia's parents," I said.

"I don't think that's a good idea, they sound insufferable. I'm imagining mother-of-the-bridezilla on steroids," Marigold hissed.

Glancing into the spare room I was shocked to see a blotchy faced Cynthia packing her suitcases, only pausing to mop up the tears. It could mean only one thing: Cynthia must have had another bridezilla meltdown, leading the two lovebirds to have a monumental row. It appeared obvious that with Cynthia simultaneously sobbing and packing her bags, the wedding must be off. I hoped that Nikos wouldn't make a fuss about returning the deposit I'd handed over for the wedding breakfast.

As Cynthia dragged her suitcases out of the bedroom I decided to intervene. "Cynthia, don't be so hasty, all couples have their ups and downs, but there's no need to call off the wedding."

"Whatever are you talking about Victor?" Marigold asked before Cynthia could get a word in edgeways. "Has Barry said something to you about having second thoughts?"

"No, I haven't spoken to Barry all day, but the

suitcases, the tears, it's obvious." Lowering my voice I hissed, "Has she pulled another bridezilla act?"

"Only if you consider refusing to share a bed with Violet Burke is pulling a bridezilla," Marigold replied.

Bravely sniffing back her tears Cynthia interjected. "Victor, you've got the wrong end of the stick. I've been so caught up in work and planning the wedding that I'd never given a thought to the sleeping arrangements here when your family arrives tomorrow. When Marigold mentioned that Barry would need to move out of the spare bedroom and onto the sofa, and that I'd have to share the bed with Violet Burke, I decided to accept Edna's offer to stay in their spare room until the wedding. Edna extended an invitation the other evening at Doreen's dinner. She thought it was bad luck to sleep under the same roof as Barry before we tie the knot."

"Surely that's only the night before the wedding," I said.

"Yes, but that was before I knew the only way to fit everyone in here was to bunk up with Violet Burke. It makes sense if I move out now Victor, Barry is going to be on the sofa and I can't see your mother willingly sharing her bed with me.

If I'm honest I don't think she took to me."

"And Milton and Edna don't strike me as the type to object if Barry sneaks over and sleeps with you there," Marigold added. "Your parents are staying in a hotel on the coast so you don't need to worry about them coming over all disapproving if Barry dares to budge from the sofa."

"It will certainly give us more room if you stay with them, and put less pressure on the queue for the bathroom," I agreed. "And you'll both be moving out anyway on the day of the wedding."

I was very relieved that the marriage was still on and agreed it made perfect sense for Cynthia to move out until the wedding, reducing the demand for the bathroom from seven to six. Out of the corner of my eye I noticed Cynthia's mutant cat boldly slinking across the salon as though it owned the place. I suppressed a howl of delight at the prospect of ejecting the vile creature alongside its owner.

"I take it those must be tears of happiness then," I said, surprised that Cynthia had recommenced her bawling.

Between strangled sobs she stuttered, "I'm just upset that I have to leave the cat behind. You don't mind holding onto Kouneli until we move into Harold's house, do you? Edna said her invitation doesn't extend to my cat since her own felines are terrified of Kouneli. I can't understand it, he's such a sweetheart."

"Have a drink with me Victor," Barry invited, dragging me over to sit on the wall in the shade of the church. Easing ourselves onto the warm stones we basked in the early evening silence, appreciating the magnificent sunset. It was a sight that never grew old. Pulling a plastic bottle of red wine and a paper cup out of a Lidl carrier bag, Barry said, "Goodness knows what this tastes like, Milton made it himself."

"I say old chap, British *spitiko*," I quipped.

We were returning home after helping Cynthia to carry her suitcases over to her temporary lodgings. Milton had given Barry the wink, indicating he was welcome to sneak in later instead of pretending to sleep on our sofa. It was no surprise that the local master of erotica wasn't prudish about having the lovebirds under his roof, though Barry would keep up the sofa pretence to appease the new in-laws. We were in no hurry to return home, Marigold still being in the throes of a manic clean up that put my own hygiene obsession to shame.

"No regrets Barry?" I asked, curious if his move to Greece and imminent marriage had made him happy.

"None at all, it's the start of a whole new chapter. Working with Vangelis is marvellous and Cynthia is made up about her promotion. It won't feel odd for you, having her as your boss?"

"I'm sure we'll rub along nicely," I said, pleased that Cynthia, knowing of my fascination with old ruins, had already suggested spicing up my excursion schedule by swapping the odd lazy day cruise with a tour of Vathia.

"This wine of Milton's isn't too bad if you ignore the sulphurous smell," Barry pronounced.

"At least we needn't worry Milton had his feet in it, I don't suppose one treads old potato peelings."

"It's quite dry. I wouldn't recommend it to any stunted flatulent tourists," Barry laughed.

"It's a big day tomorrow, meeting the in-laws for the first time," I reminded him.

"I know. I wish Cynthia could come up to the airport with me to collect them, but she's flat out at work. I'll make a sign when we get home."

"A sign?"

"With their name on. Trout. I don't want them getting their hopes up thinking some handsome Greek type hanging round the arrivals area is me, best if I flash a sign as soon as their plane lands so there's no misunderstandings. How about you, how are you feeling about seeing Violet Burke again?"

"I'm actually looking forward to the chance to get to know her. It's you who has the big week ahead Barry, getting married and moving into a new home."

"If you'd said a year ago that all this would be happening, flitting from Manchester to Meli, and meeting the woman I'm about to marry, I'd have said you were bonkers," Barry chuckled.

"You could have said I was round the bend…"

"But you never know what's round the bend." Barry grinned, nudging me in the ribs.

"And you're sure about Harold's house?"

"We'll get Papas Andreas round to wave his sprig of basil and expunge all trace of Harold and Joan," Barry said. "The icing on the cake is that you and Marigold are just round the corner."

"Any pre-wedding nerves?" I asked.

"Funnily enough, no. I did have just the one wobble, but then I remembered you'd be standing right beside me as my best man."

"Always. Let's toast to that," I said, raising the paper cup. "Here's to many long and happy years in Greece. *Yamas*."

"*Yamas*."

The moment of brotherly camaraderie was marred by a pesky mosquito buzzing around Barry's exposed bits.

"I forgot to douse myself with vinegar, it won't be a good look if I'm covered with angry red bites in the wedding pictures," Barry sighed.

"Here, take the bottle and rub some of Milton's potato plonk in. I doubt the mossies will survive a close encounter."

A Note from Victor

All Amazon reviews most welcome.
Please feel free to drop a line if you would like information on the release date of future volumes in the Bucket series.

vdbucket@gmail.com

Made in the USA
Coppell, TX
02 June 2023

17622615R00174